Holidays In Cross-Stitch volume 2

OXMOOR HOUSE, INC.
and
LEISURE ARTS, INC.

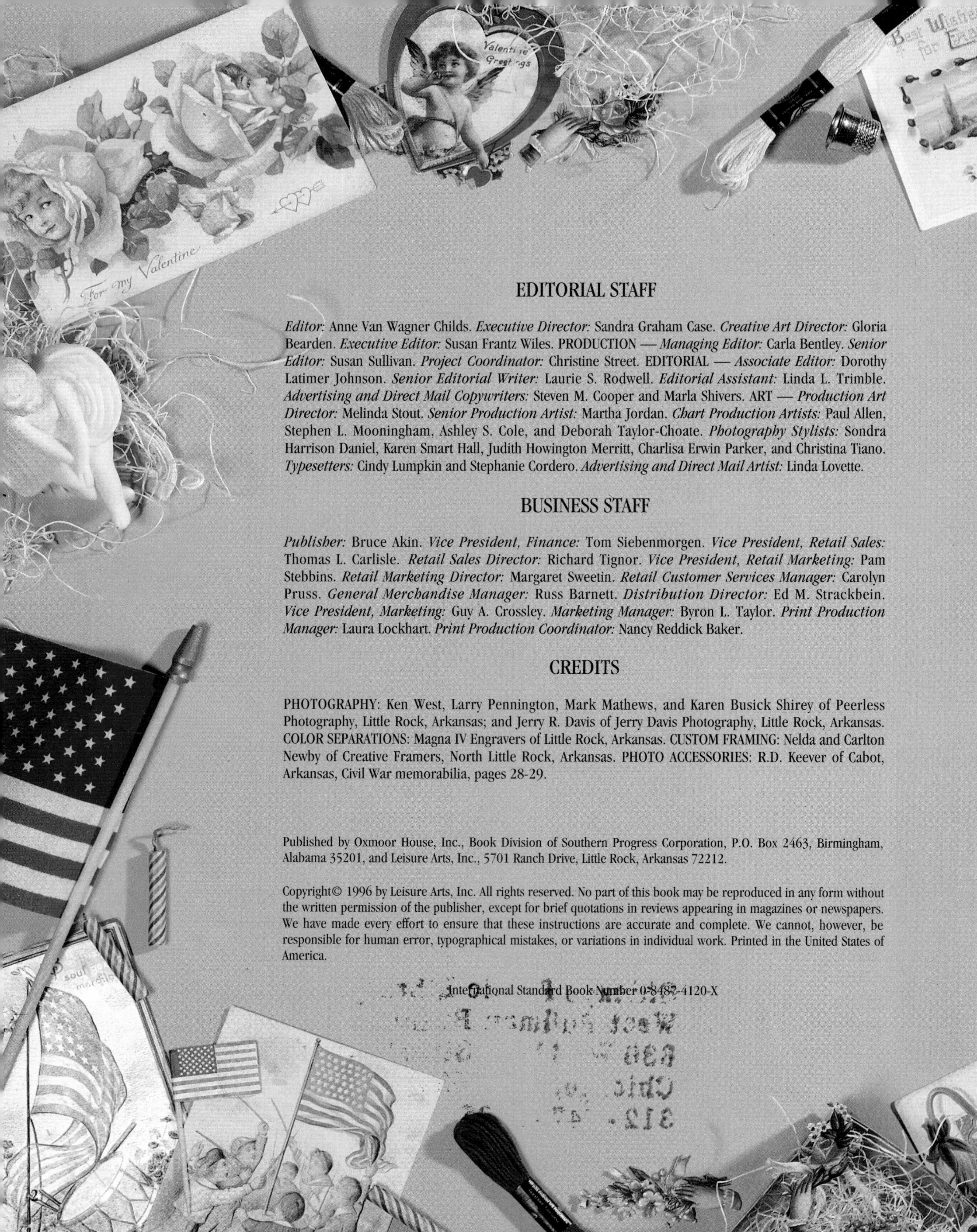

EDITORIAL STAFF

BUSINESS STAFF

CREDITS

PHOTOGRAPHY: Ken West, Larry Pennington, Mark Mathews, and Karen Busick Shirey of Peerless Photography, Little Rock, Arkansas; and Jerry R. Davis of Jerry Davis Photography, Little Rock, Arkansas. COLOR SEPARATIONS: Magna IV Engravers of Little Rock, Arkansas. CUSTOM FRAMING: Nelda and Carlton Newby of Creative Framers, North Little Rock, Arkansas. PHOTO ACCESSORIES: R.D. Keever of Cabot, Arkansas, Civil War memorabilia, pages 28-29.

Published by Oxmoor House, Inc., Book Division of Southern Progress Corporation, P.O. Box 2463, Birmingham, Alabama 35201, and Leisure Arts, Inc., 5701 Ranch Drive, Little Rock, Arkansas 72212.

International Standard Book Number 0-8487-4120-X

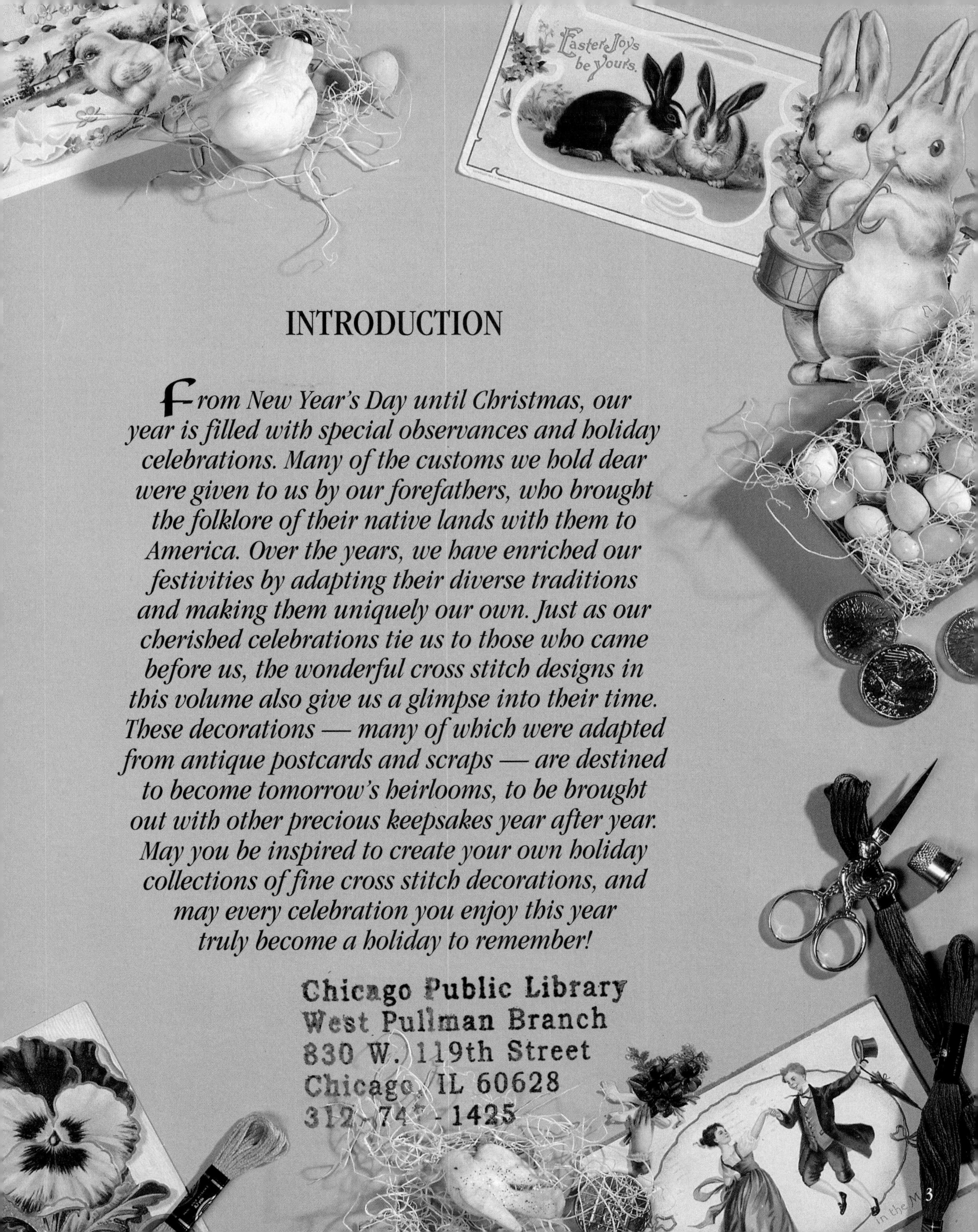

INTRODUCTION

From New Year's Day until Christmas, our year is filled with special observances and holiday celebrations. Many of the customs we hold dear were given to us by our forefathers, who brought the folklore of their native lands with them to America. Over the years, we have enriched our festivities by adapting their diverse traditions and making them uniquely our own. Just as our cherished celebrations tie us to those who came before us, the wonderful cross stitch designs in this volume also give us a glimpse into their time. These decorations — many of which were adapted from antique postcards and scraps — are destined to become tomorrow's heirlooms, to be brought out with other precious keepsakes year after year. May you be inspired to create your own holiday collections of fine cross stitch decorations, and may every celebration you enjoy this year truly become a holiday to remember!

TABLE OF CONTENTS

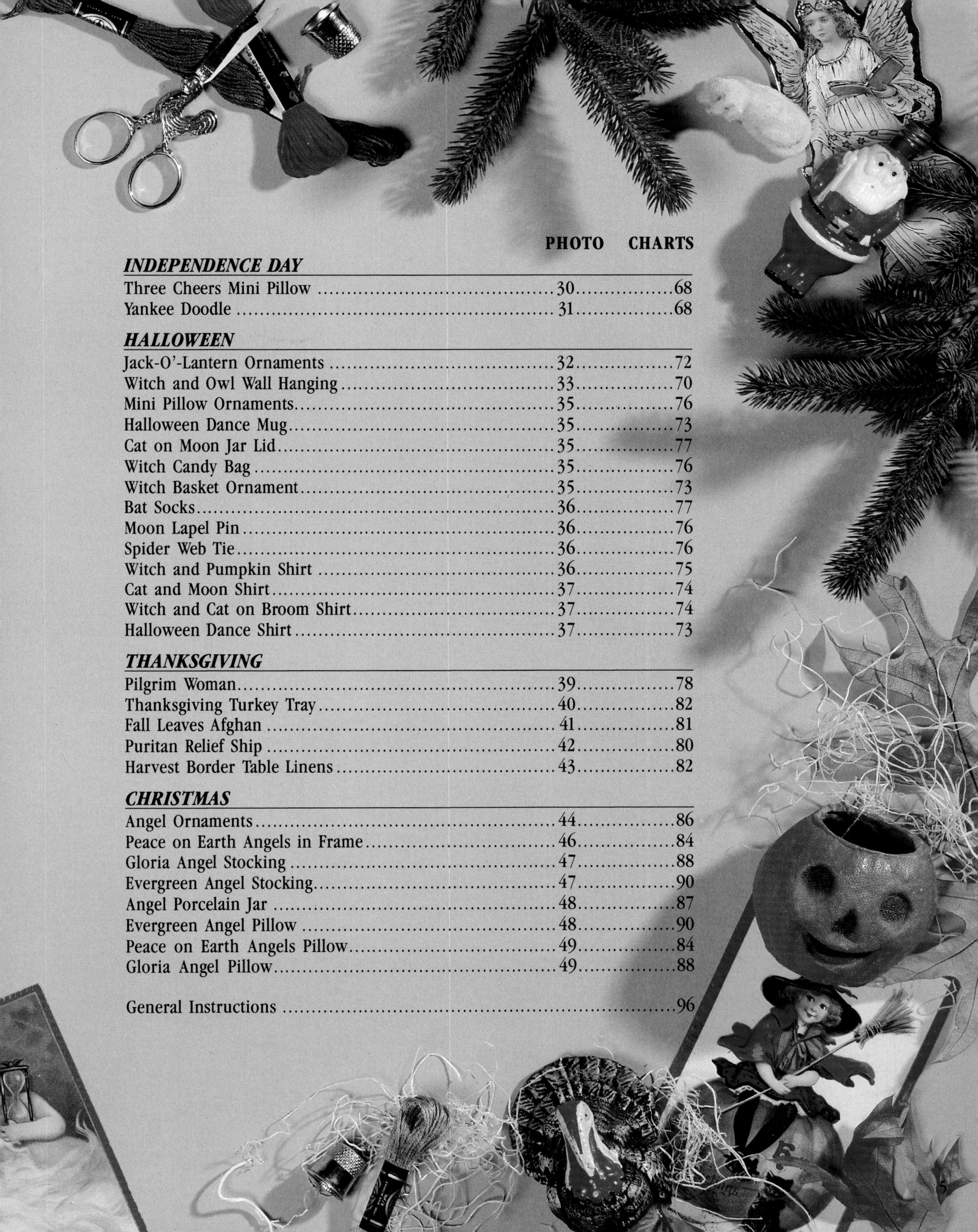

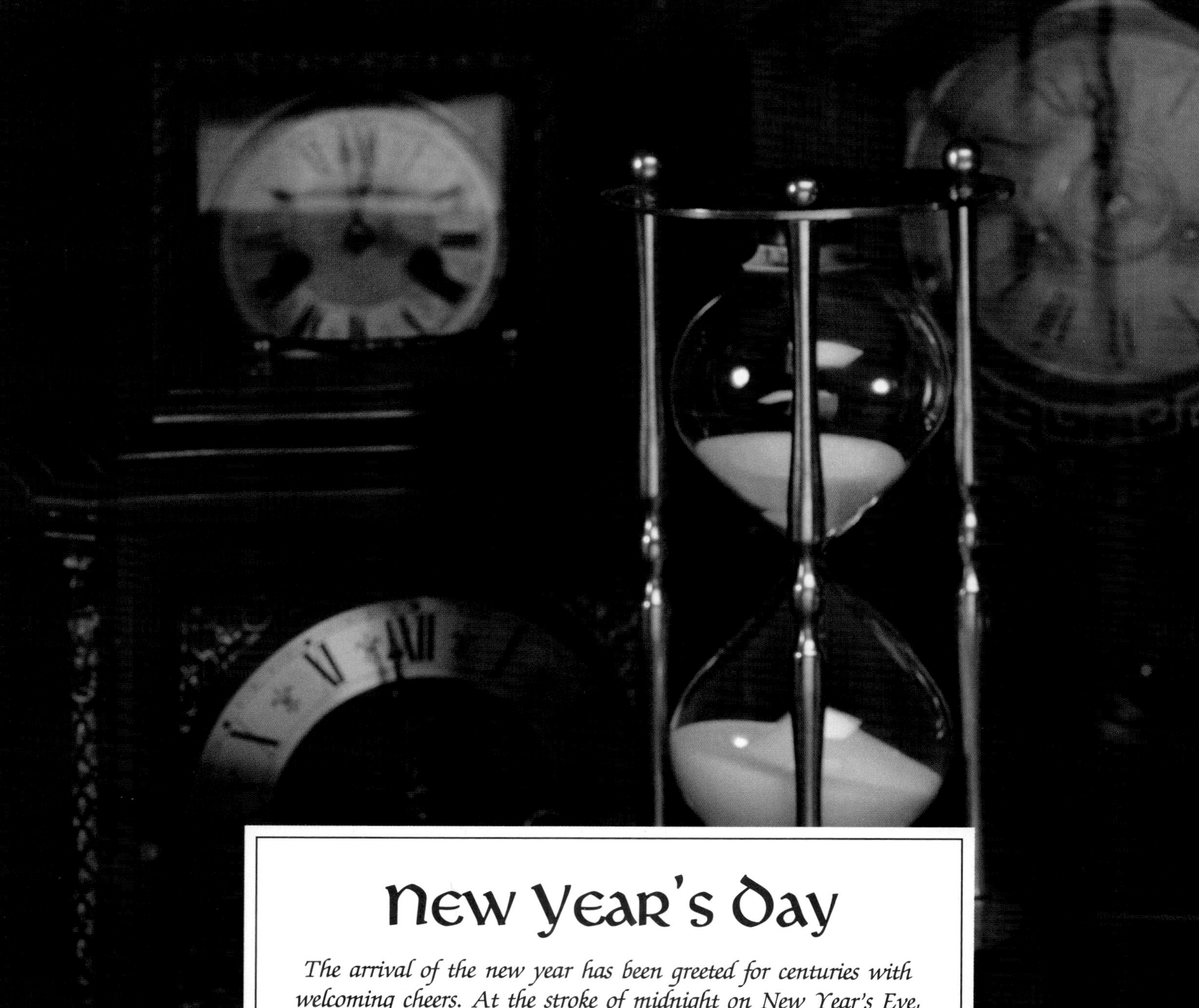

New Year's Day

The arrival of the new year has been greeted for centuries with welcoming cheers. At the stroke of midnight on New Year's Eve, laughter reigns as we exchange hugs, kisses, and wishes for health and happiness. For in its infancy, the new year reminds us of the potential of the future, filling us with a delightful sense of hope and expectation on this most promising of holidays.

Chart on page 50

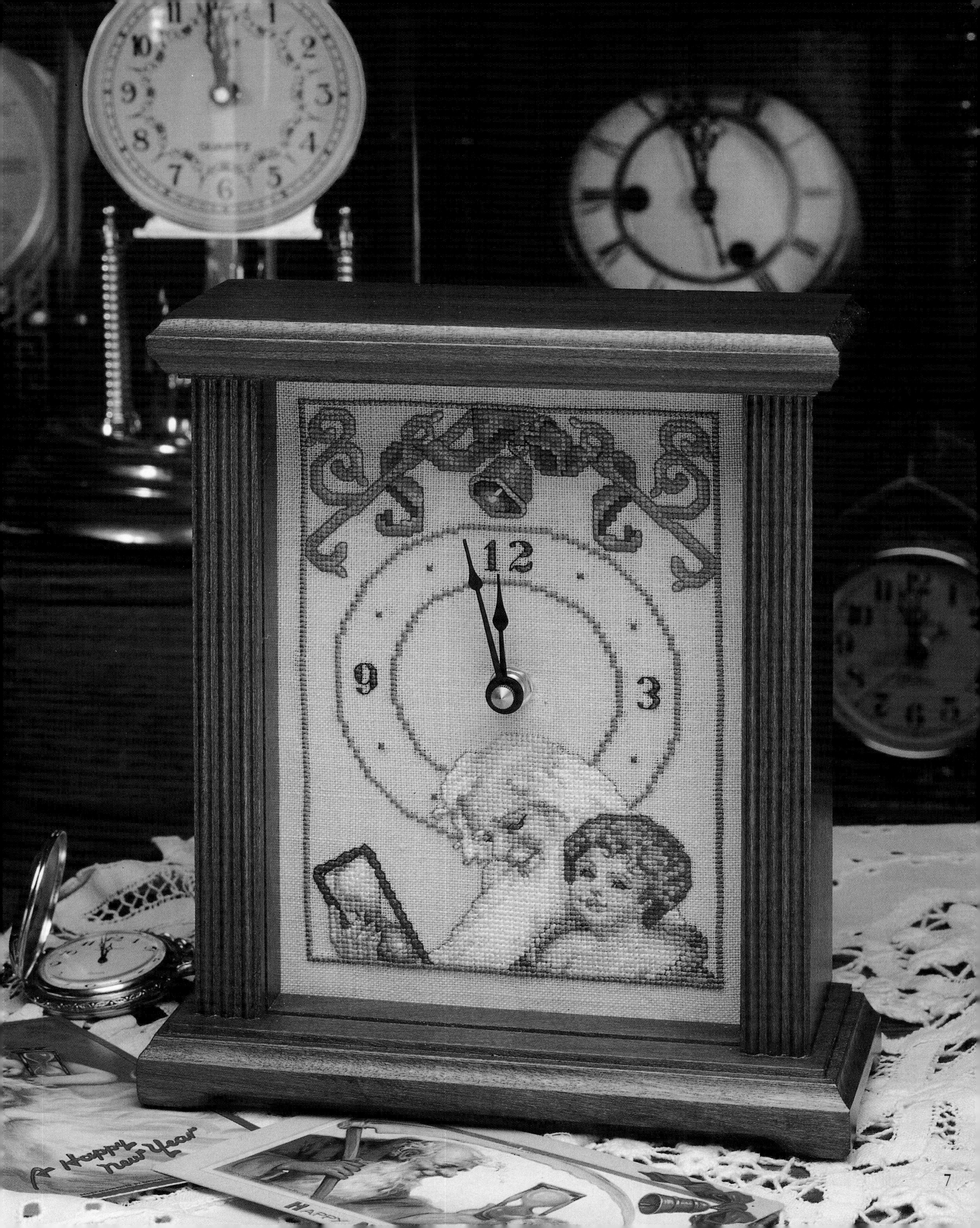
12
9
3
A Happy New Year

Valentine's Day

Dedicated to romance, St. Valentine's Day has always been the favorite holiday of lovers. To express their affection for one another on this special day, sweethearts freely exchange cards, gifts, and other tokens of esteem. These heartfelt declarations of devotion are tender testimonials to the power of love!

Chart on page 54

Cupids, turtledoves, roses, and hearts — these are the emblems of love that have adorned valentines throughout the years. In this beautiful collection, these timeless images have been captured with needle and thread to create sentimental accents and accessories, all destined to become tomorrow's treasures.

A Marriage Blessing
Look down with favor, O Lord,
On these Thy children,
Who by Thy divine authority
Are one in holy matrimony.
Grant them Thy protection
Through days of lasting peace
And bless them with the love
Of their children's children.
Amen

Chart on page 55

Charts on pages 52-53

Chart on page 54

Charts on page 51

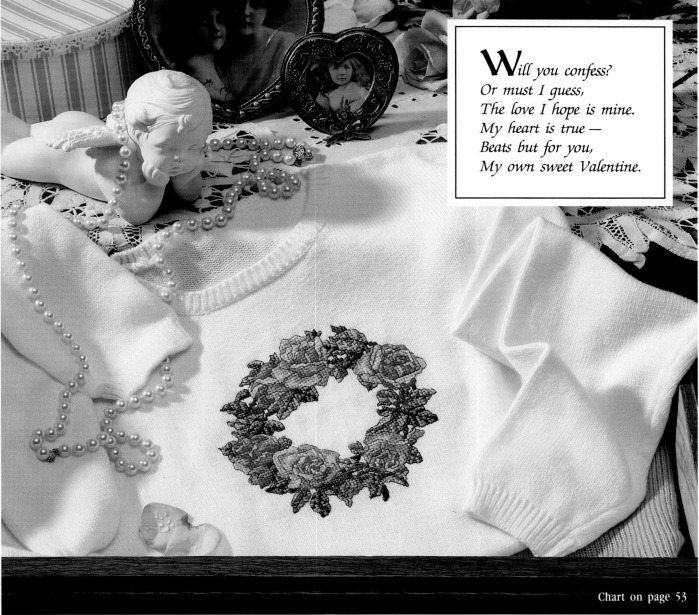

Will you confess?
Or must I guess,
The love I hope is mine.
My heart is true —
Beats but for you,
My own sweet Valentine.

Chart on page 53

Presidents' Day

Revered by young and old alike, George Washington and Abraham Lincoln will ever symbolize this country's proud heritage of independence and freedom. As our first president, Washington guided the colonies through the dark days of the American Revolution. It was Lincoln's leadership in the White House that prevented the Civil War from forever dividing the United States. In recent years, instead of celebrating Lincoln's birthday on February 12 and Washington's birthday on February 22, we honor both on Presidents' Day — the third Monday in February.

Charts on page 56

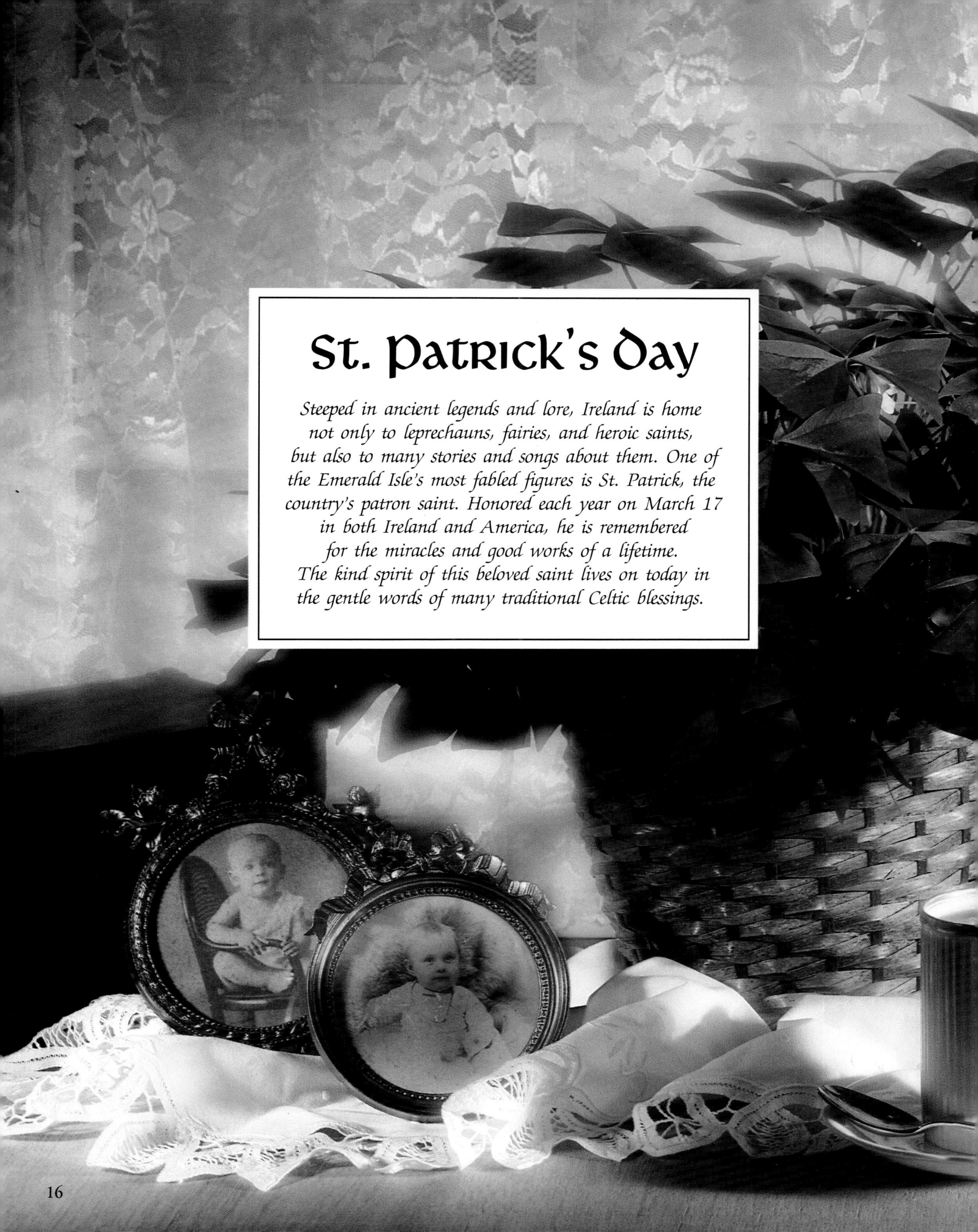

St. Patrick's Day

Steeped in ancient legends and lore, Ireland is home not only to leprechauns, fairies, and heroic saints, but also to many stories and songs about them. One of the Emerald Isle's most fabled figures is St. Patrick, the country's patron saint. Honored each year on March 17 in both Ireland and America, he is remembered for the miracles and good works of a lifetime. The kind spirit of this beloved saint lives on today in the gentle words of many traditional Celtic blessings.

May the most
you wish for
Be the least
you get...
May the best times
you've ever had
Be the worst
you will ever see...
OLD CELTIC BLESSING

Chart on page 57

Easter

One of the most joyous celebrations of the year, Easter embraces both the Resurrection's promise of eternal life and the rebirth we see in nature each spring. This charming collection captures many of the beloved images that make this holiday so special. Today, as in the past, bunnies and chicks, colored eggs, and spring flowers enchant both children and adults at Eastertime.

Chart on pages 58-59

On Easter morning what an excitement there is to see what the good little hare has brought! Not only real eggs boiled and colored, but sugar ones too, and often wooden ones that open like boxes, disclosing, perhaps, a pair of new gloves or a bright ribbon. He even sometimes brings hoops and skipping-ropes, and generally his own effigy in dough or candy is found trying to scamper away behind the nest.

— F.E. CORNE

Chart on page 64

Chart on page 63

Charts on page 64

Chart on page 61

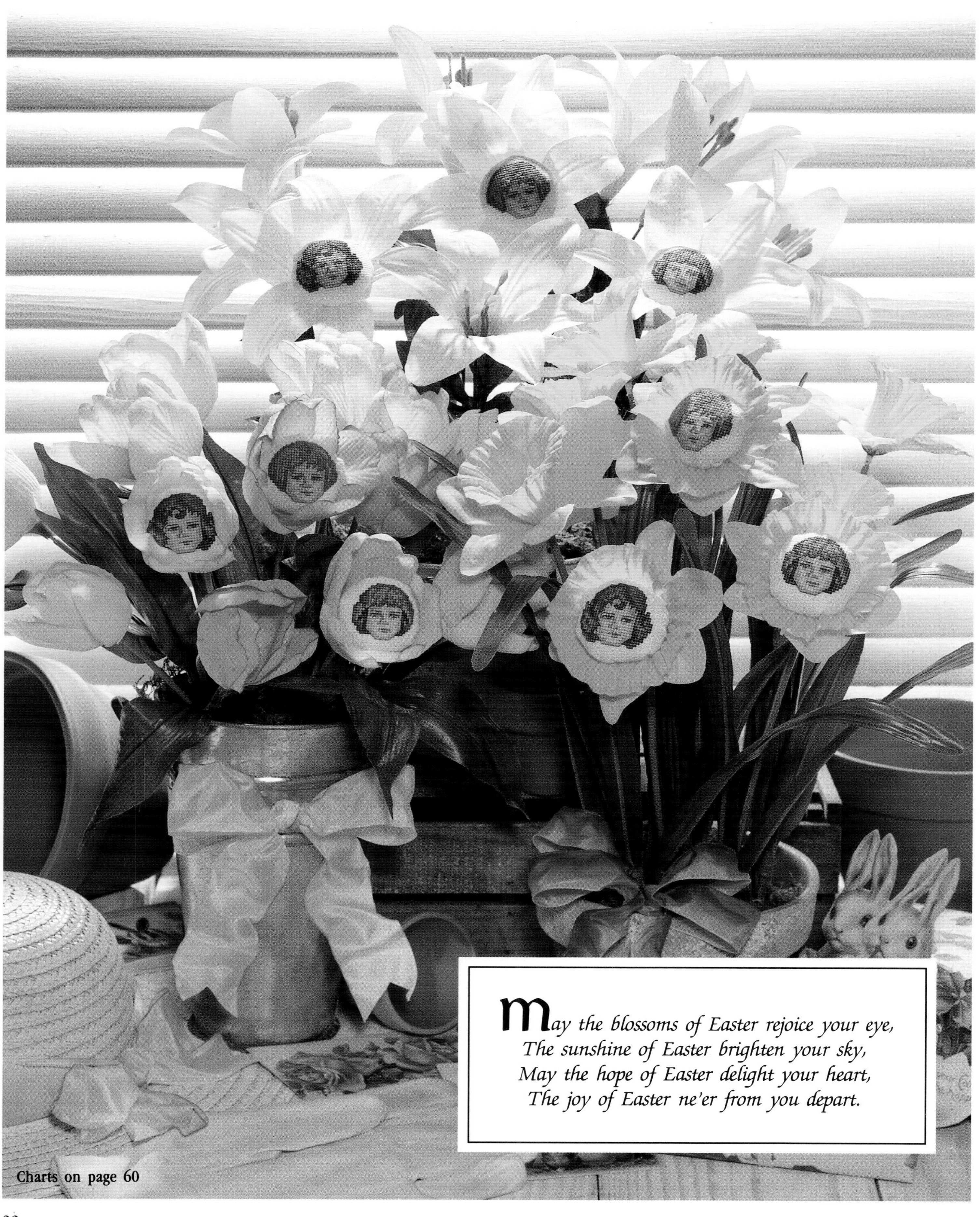

May the blossoms of Easter rejoice your eye,
The sunshine of Easter brighten your sky,
May the hope of Easter delight your heart,
The joy of Easter ne'er from you depart.

Charts on page 60

Charts on pages 61-62

Chart on page 93

May Day

Warm, sunny weather and May Day often arrive hand in hand, and we find ourselves enticed outdoors to enjoy the fragrance and beauty of our flower gardens. Fulfilling the season's eternal promise of renewal, each dainty new blossom lifts our spirits. The pretty pansies and violets in this collection are lovely year-round reminders of spring. Drawn with delicate precision, illustrations such as the ones from which these designs were adapted are a wonderful legacy left to us by turn-of-the-century artists. Their timeless tributes to the splendor of spring flowers have been preserved on postcards and scraps, and in the bright, colorful seed catalogs that were so popular then.

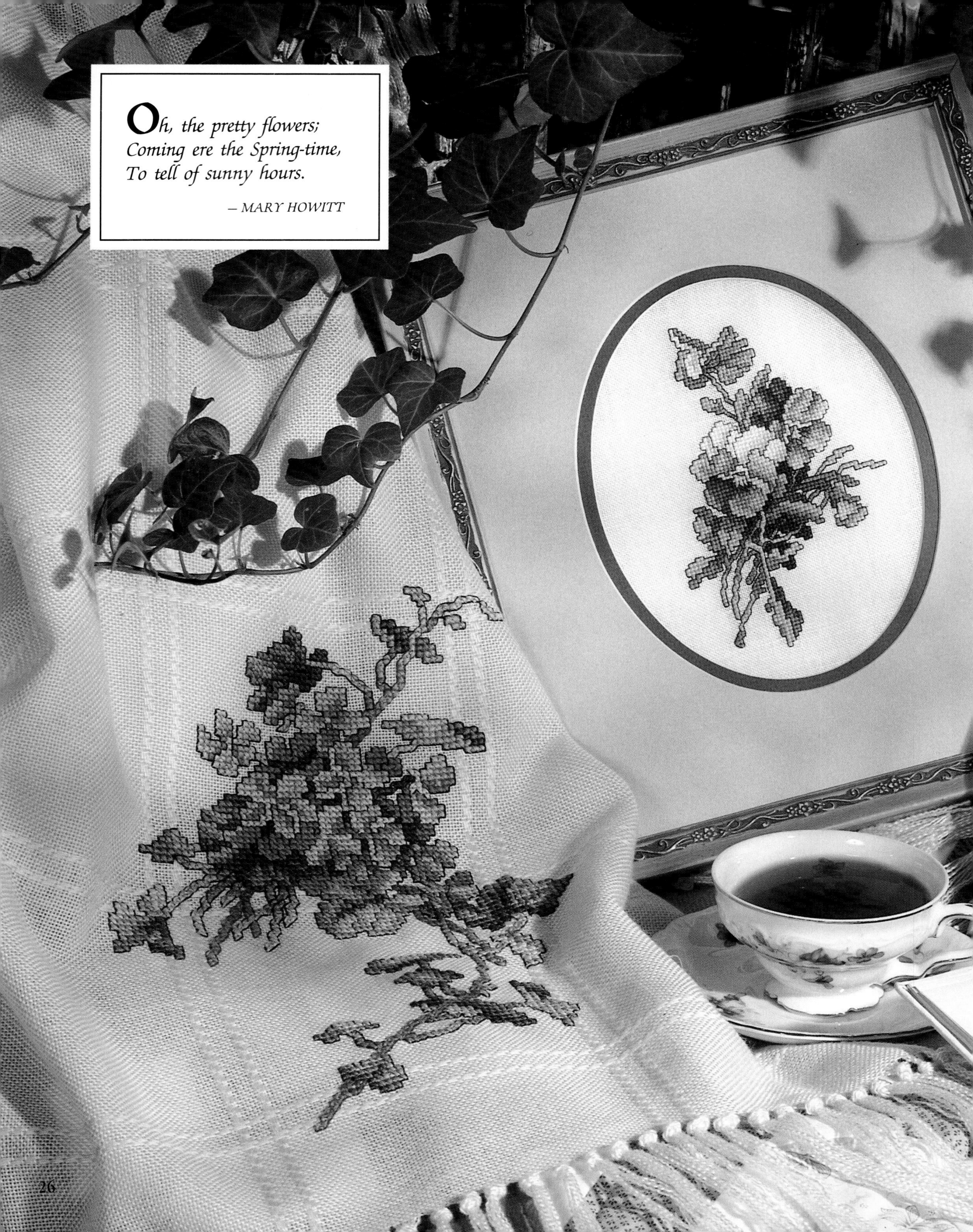
Oh, the pretty flowers;
Coming ere the Spring-time,
To tell of sunny hours.
– MARY HOWITT

Charts on pages 94-95

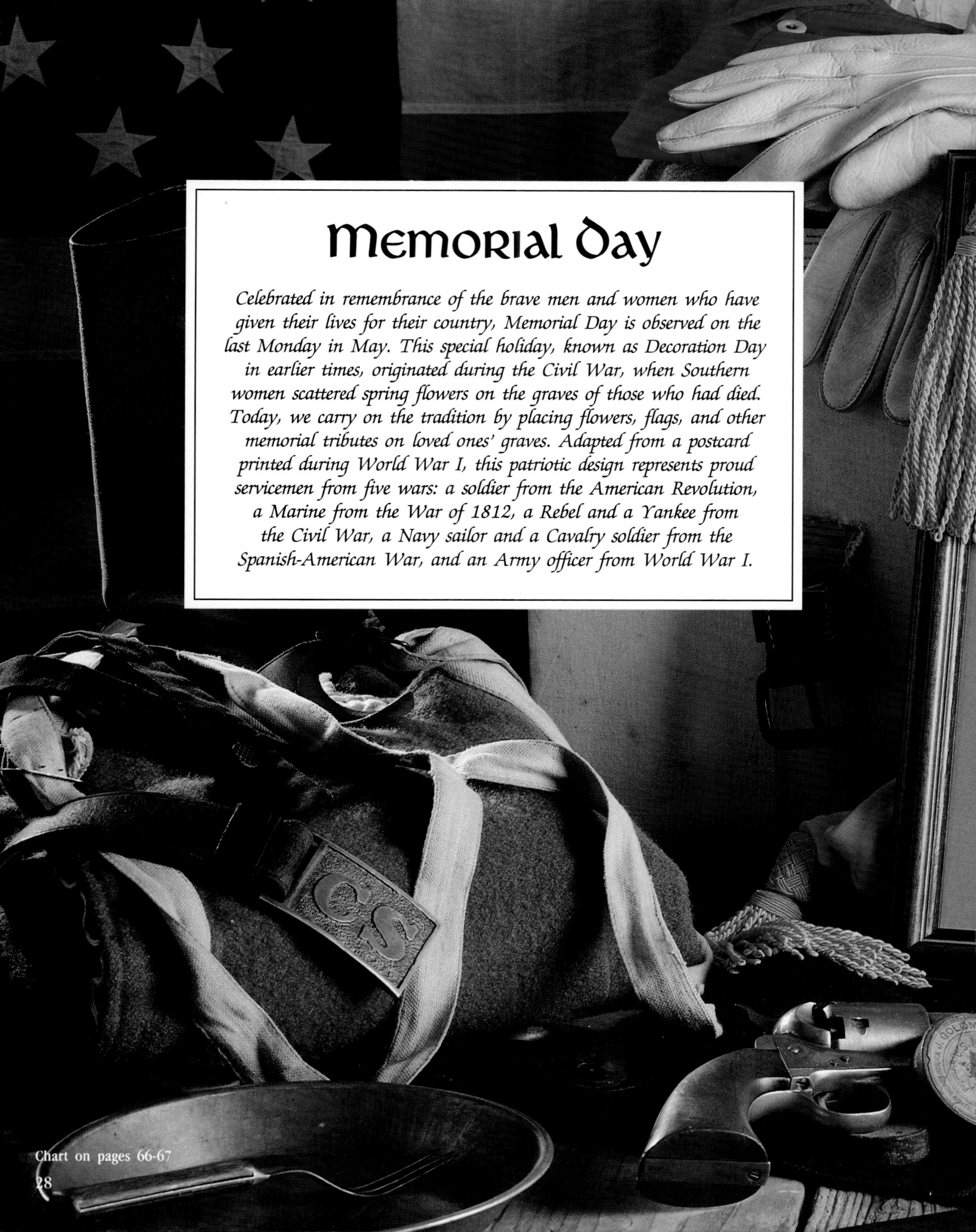

Memorial Day

Celebrated in remembrance of the brave men and women who have given their lives for their country, Memorial Day is observed on the last Monday in May. This special holiday, known as Decoration Day in earlier times, originated during the Civil War, when Southern women scattered spring flowers on the graves of those who had died. Today, we carry on the tradition by placing flowers, flags, and other memorial tributes on loved ones' graves. Adapted from a postcard printed during World War I, this patriotic design represents proud servicemen from five wars: a soldier from the American Revolution, a Marine from the War of 1812, a Rebel and a Yankee from the Civil War, a Navy sailor and a Cavalry soldier from the Spanish-American War, and an Army officer from World War I.

Chart on pages 66-67

One flag, one land,
one heart, one hand,
One Nation, "Evermore!"

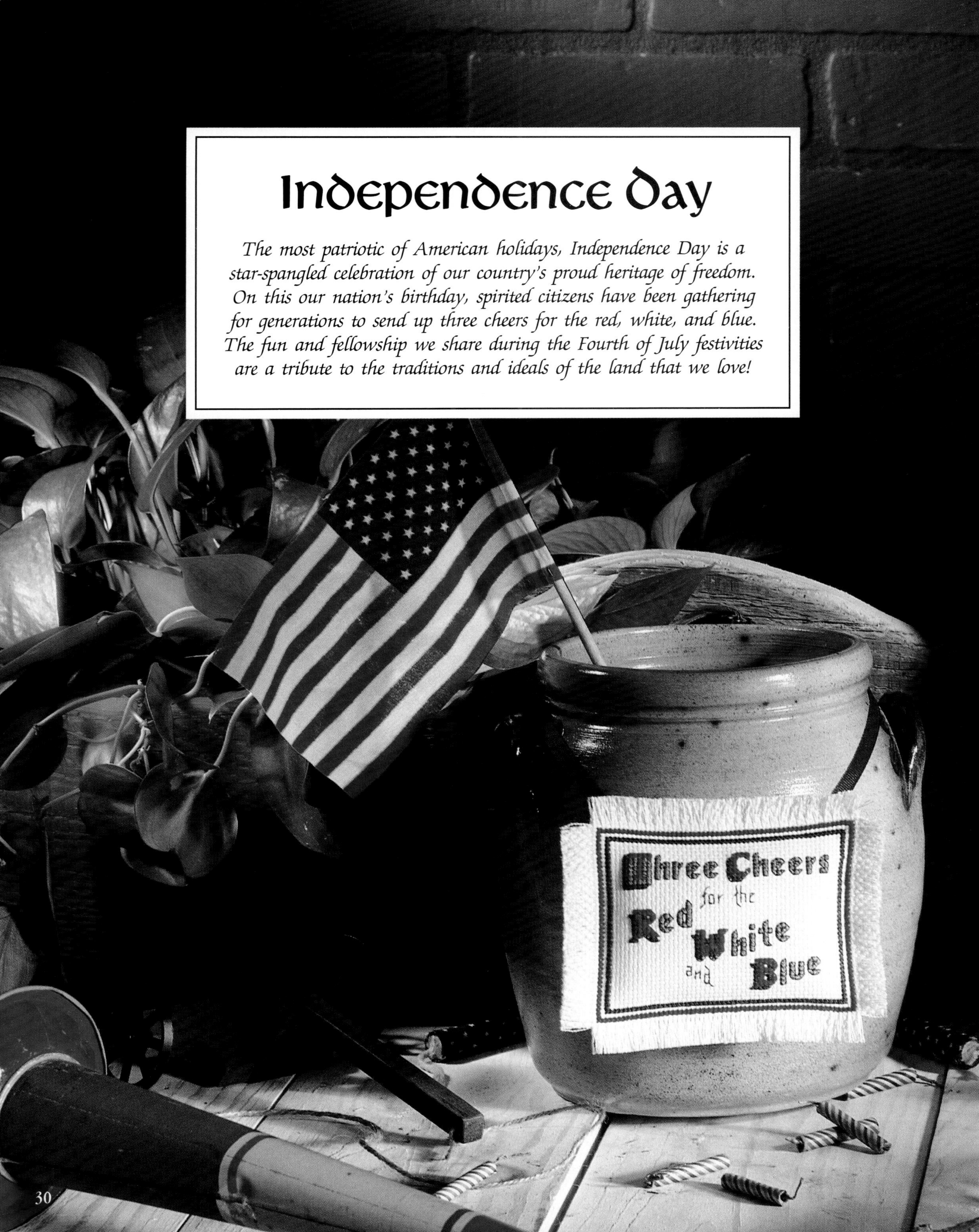
Three Cheers
for the
Red
White
and
Blue

Independence Day

The most patriotic of American holidays, Independence Day is a star-spangled celebration of our country's proud heritage of freedom. On this our nation's birthday, spirited citizens have been gathering for generations to send up three cheers for the red, white, and blue. The fun and fellowship we share during the Fourth of July festivities are a tribute to the traditions and ideals of the land that we love!

Charts on pages

halloween

On Halloween, the eve of All Saints' Day, ghosts and other spirits were once believed to roam about, their paths illuminated by the light of glowing jack-o'-lanterns. As superstitions weakened over the centuries, these goblins took on a more playful look, inspiring frightfully delightful postcard art such as that from which these designs were adapted.

Charts on page 72

When the Owl
& Witch
together are seen,
there's mischief brewing
on Hallowe'en.

In times gone by, people gathered for reassurance on this bewitching night. They passed the evening by telling ghost stories, bobbing for apples, and playing other games. Today, the spooky parties, frightful decorations, and scary costumes that we so enjoy all reflect the superstitious origins of this haunting holiday.

Charts on page 72

Charts on pages 76-77

Charts on pages 73 and 76-77

Charts on pages 76-77

Chart on page 75

To scare away the frightening spirits that they believed were out on Halloween, our ancestors in Ireland donned terrifying costumes and masks. By the time the custom was introduced to Americans by Irish immigrants, it had become a fun-filled opportunity for people to indulge their imaginations. Today, masquerading remains a popular tradition on October 31.

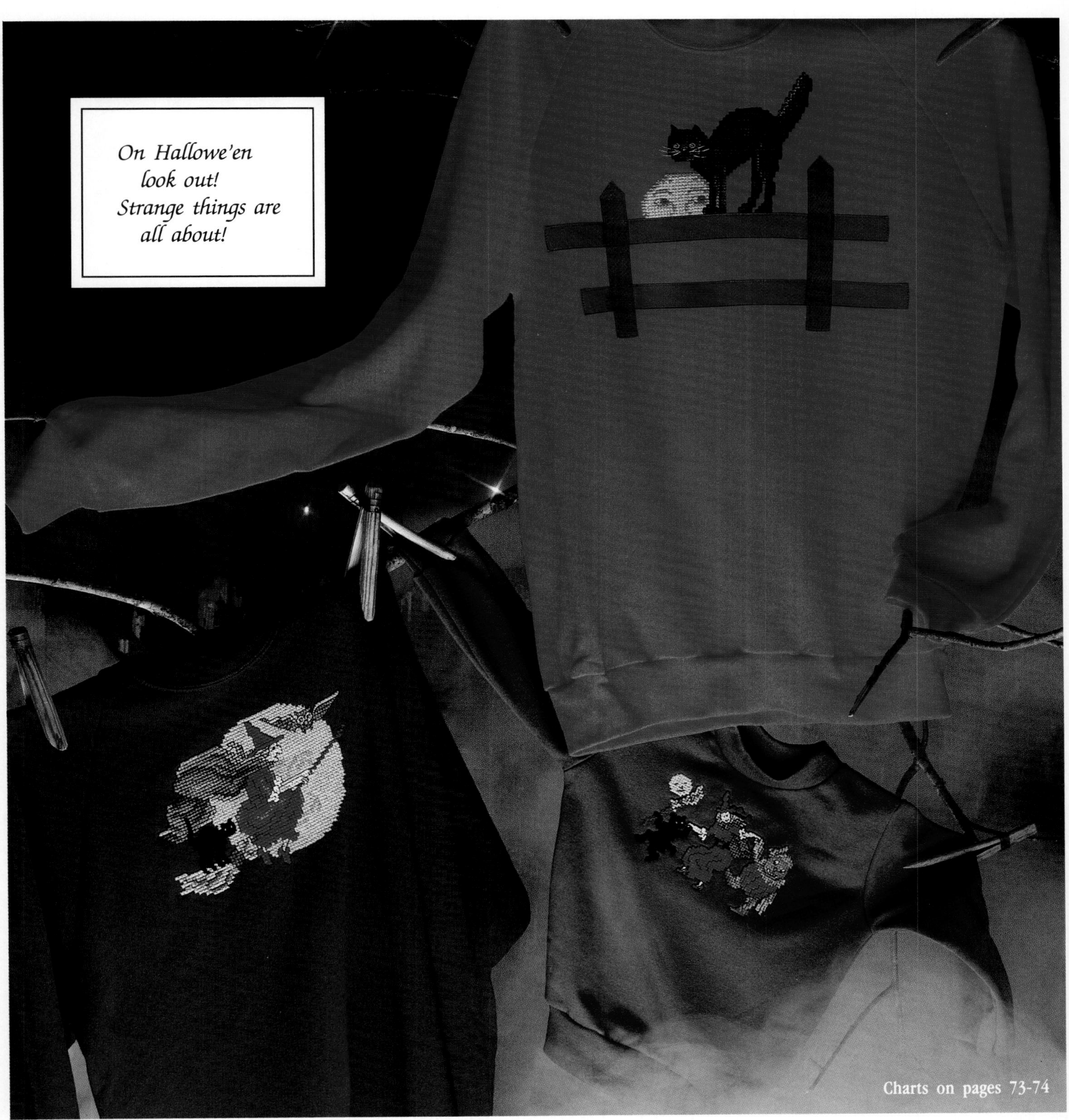

On Hallowe'en
look out!
Strange things are
all about!

Charts on pages 73-74

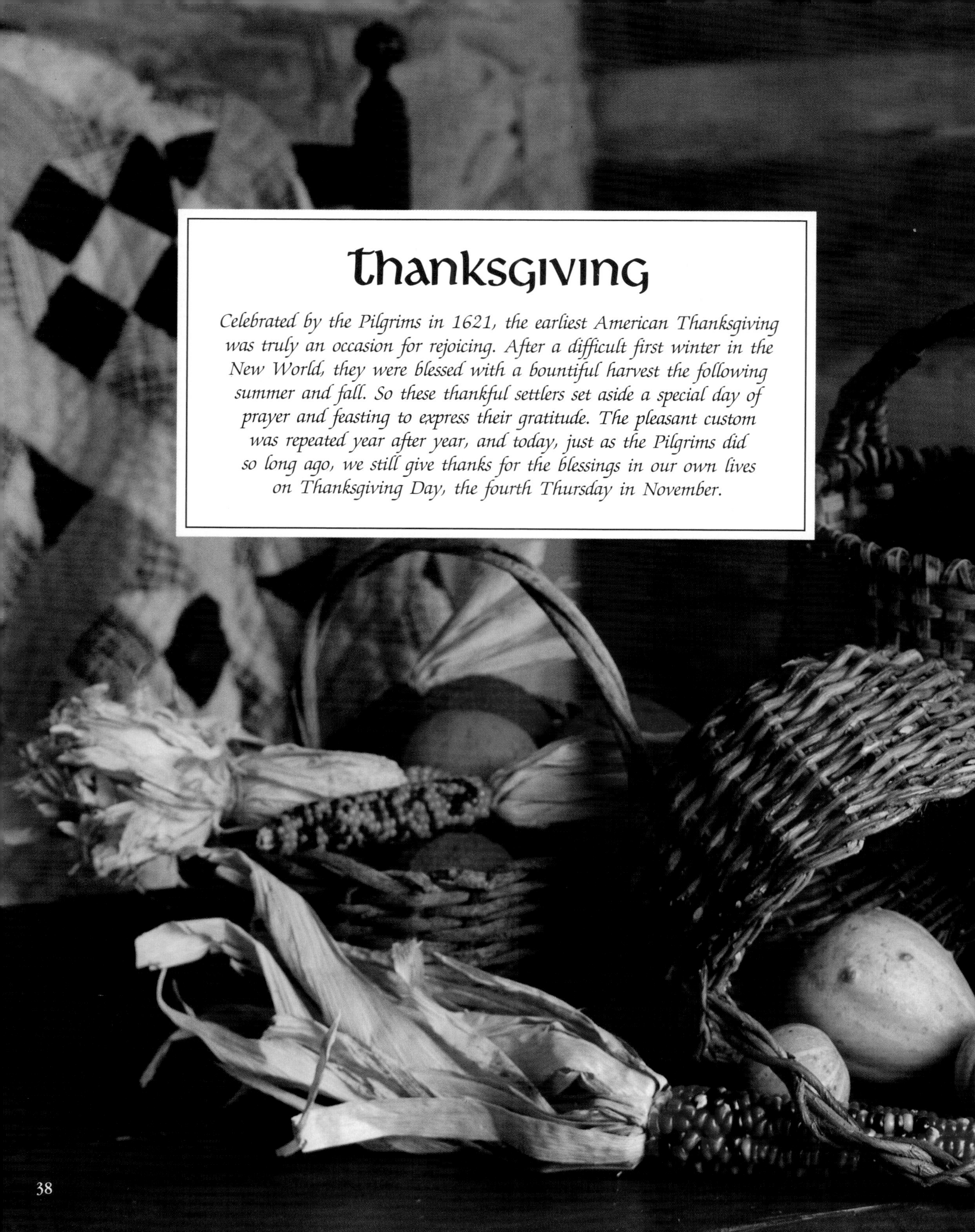

Thanksgiving

Celebrated by the Pilgrims in 1621, the earliest American Thanksgiving was truly an occasion for rejoicing. After a difficult first winter in the New World, they were blessed with a bountiful harvest the following summer and fall. So these thankful settlers set aside a special day of prayer and feasting to express their gratitude. The pleasant custom was repeated year after year, and today, just as the Pilgrims did so long ago, we still give thanks for the blessings in our own lives on Thanksgiving Day, the fourth Thursday in November.

Chart on pages 78-79

Chart on pages 82-83

Family and friends are one of life's greatest gifts, and sharing our Thanksgiving celebrations with those we love is one of the day's greatest delights. Your guests will be charmed by this serving tray featuring a plump turkey — one of the traditional symbols of this American holiday. Adorned with autumn motifs in rich harvest colors, an afghan draped invitingly across the sofa will tempt your company to linger a few moments longer as the day's festivities end.

Chart on page 81

For the Pilgrims, the arrival of a ship from Europe was always greeted with sighs of relief and prayers of thanks. Besides delivering precious supplies, the ships sometimes carried beloved friends coming to join them in America. We can just imagine the festivities that were held to honor the newcomers and to rejoice for the provisions they brought with them! In the spirit of the settlers' joyous celebrations, a table set for guests is graced by linen accessories featuring bountiful fruit and vegetable motifs.

Chart on page 80

Chart on pages 82-83

Christmas

Each December as we retell the Christmas story, we are reminded of the divine role played by angels. With their jubilant message of "Peace on earth, good will toward men," these celestial beings were the first to herald the birth of the Baby Jesus. This elegant collection honors the sweet souls sent from heaven with glad tidings of hope, joy, and love.

Charts on pages 86-87

Chart on pages 84-85

Charts on pages 84-85, 88-91

New Year's Day

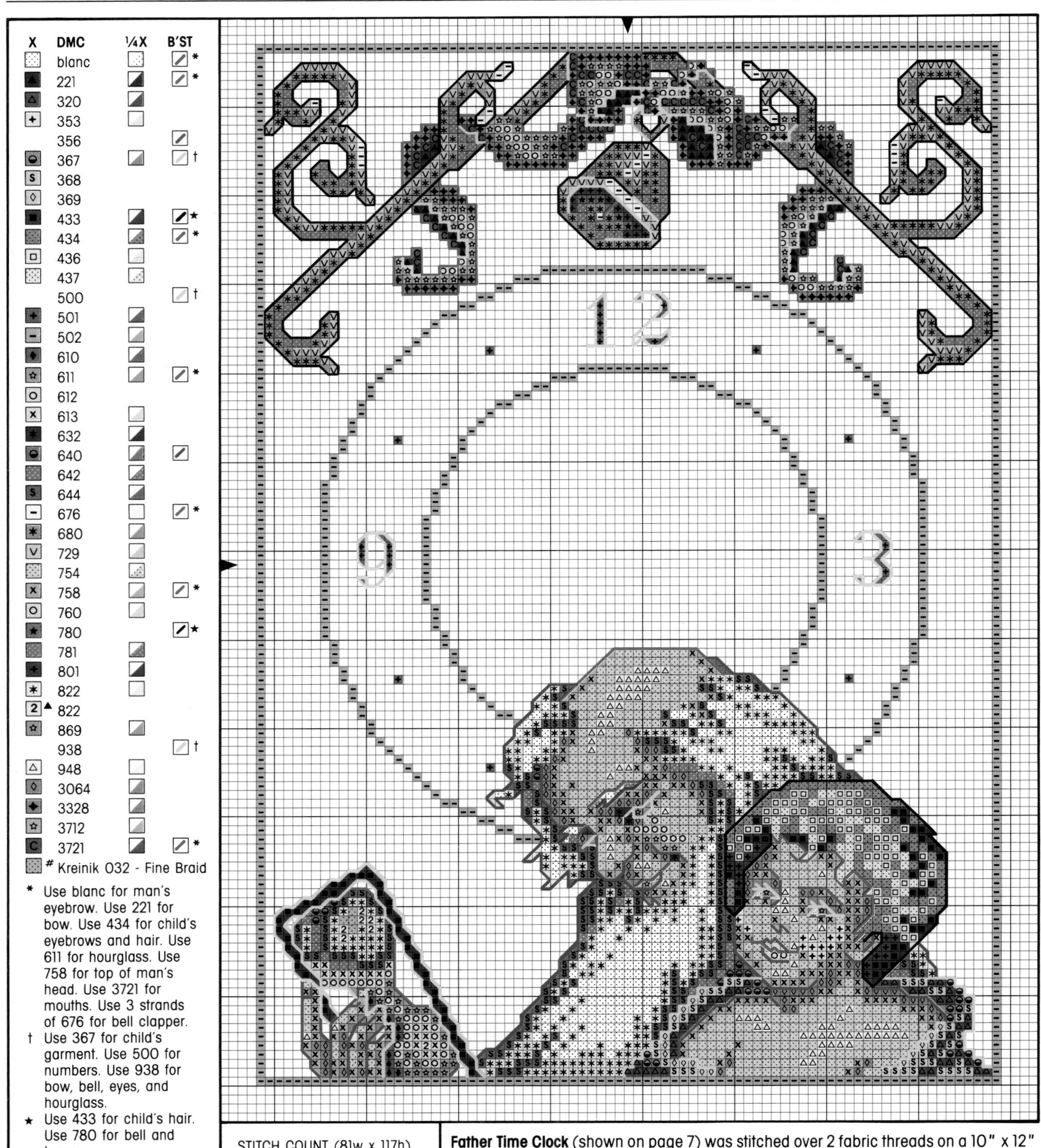

DMC	B'ST
blanc	*
221	*
320	
353	
356	
367	†
368	
369	
433	★
434	*
436	
437	
500	†
501	
502	
610	
611	*
612	
613	
632	
640	
642	
644	
676	*
680	
729	
754	
758	*
760	
780	★
781	
801	
822	
822 ▲	
869	
938	†
948	
3064	
3328	
3712	
3721	*
# Kreinik 032 - Fine Braid	

* Use blanc for man's eyebrow. Use 221 for bow. Use 434 for child's eyebrows and hair. Use 611 for hourglass. Use 758 for top of man's head. Use 3721 for mouths. Use 3 strands of 676 for bell clapper.

† Use 367 for child's garment. Use 500 for numbers. Use 938 for bow, bell, eyes, and hourglass.

★ Use 433 for child's hair. Use 780 for bell and brass.

▲ Use 1 strand of floss and 1 strand of Kreinik 032 - Fine Braid.

\# Use 1 strand of braid.

STITCH COUNT (81w x 117h)			
14 count	5⅞"	x	8⅜"
16 count	5⅛"	x	7⅜"
18 count	4½"	x	6½"
22 count	3¾"	x	5⅜"

Father Time Clock (shown on page 7) was stitched over 2 fabric threads on a 10" x 12" piece of Tea-Dyed Irish Linen (36 ct). Two strands of floss were used for Cross Stitch and 1 strand for Backstitch. It was inserted in a purchased clock (5" x 7" opening).

Needlework adaptation by Carol Emmer.

Capturing the innocence and purity of angels as we imagine them to be, these lovely designs make glorious Yuletide decorations. With their flowing robes, graceful wings, and gentle expressions, the angels here bear cherished symbols of the Christmas story.

Charts on pages 88-91

Chart on page 87

Good news from heaven
the angels bring
Glad tidings to the earth
they sing:
To us this day a child
is given,
To crown us with the joy
of heaven.

– MARTIN LUTHER

Charts on pages 84-85, 88-91

New Year's Day

X DMC ¼X B'ST
blanc *
221 *
320
353
356
367 †
368
369
433 ★
434 *
436
437
500 †
501
502
610
611 *
612
613
632
640
642
644
676 *
680
729
754
758 *
760
780 ★
781
801
822
822 ▲
869
938 †
948
3064
3328
3712
3721 *
Kreinik 032 - Fine Braid
12
9
3

* Use blanc for man's eyebrow. Use 221 for bow. Use 434 for child's eyebrows and hair. Use 611 for hourglass. Use 758 for top of man's head. Use 3721 for mouths. Use 3 strands of 676 for bell clapper.

† Use 367 for child's garment. Use 500 for numbers. Use 938 for bow, bell, eyes, and hourglass.

★ Use 433 for child's hair. Use 780 for bell and brass.

▲ Use 1 strand of floss and 1 strand of Kreinik 032 - Fine Braid.

Use 1 strand of braid.

STITCH COUNT (81w x 117h)

14 count	5⅞"	x	8⅜"
16 count	5⅛"	x	7⅜"
18 count	4½"	x	6½"
22 count	3¾"	x	5⅜"

Father Time Clock (shown on page 7) was stitched over 2 fabric threads on a 10" x 12" piece of Tea-Dyed Irish Linen (36 ct). Two strands of floss were used for Cross Stitch and 1 strand for Backstitch. It was inserted in a purchased clock (5" x 7" opening).

Needlework adaptation by Carol Emmer.

Valentine's Day

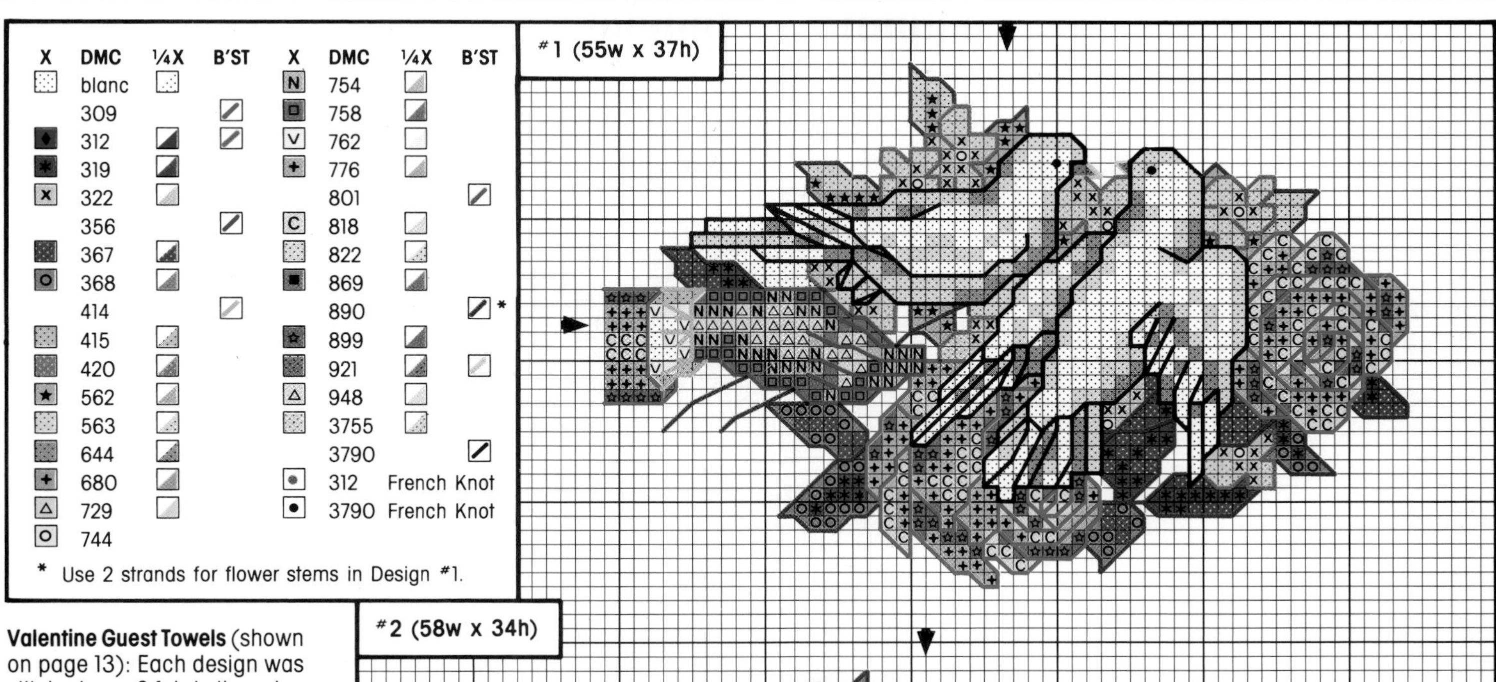

X	DMC	1/4X	B'ST	X	DMC	1/4X	B'ST
·	blanc	/		N	754	/	
	309		/	□	758	/	
♦	312	/	/	V	762	/	
✱	319	/		+	776	/	
×	322	/			801		/
	356		/	C	818	/	
	367	/			822	/	
○	368	/		■	869	/	
	414		/		890		/*
	415	/		☆	899	/	
	420	/			921	/	/
★	562	/		△	948	/	
	563	/			3755	/	
	644	/			3790		/
+	680	/		●	312 French Knot		
△	729	/		●	3790 French Knot		
○	744						

* Use 2 strands for flower stems in Design #1.

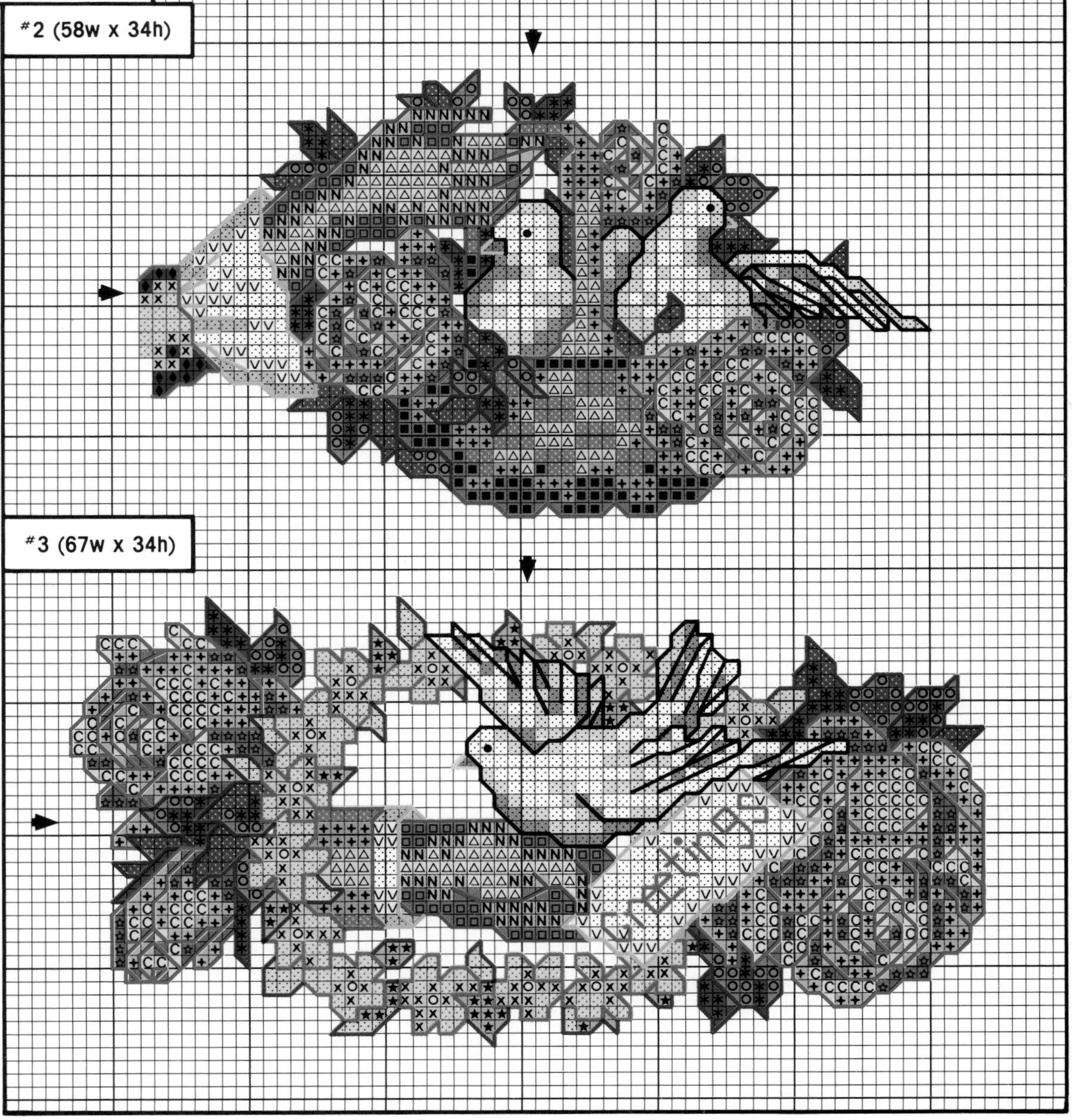

#2 (58w x 34h)

#3 (67w x 34h)

Valentine Guest Towels (shown on page 13): Each design was stitched over 2 fabric threads on a 12" x 20" piece of White Belfast Linen (32 ct) with bottom of design 1¼" from one short edge of fabric. Two strands of floss were used for Cross Stitch and 1 strand for all other stitches. They were made into towels.

For each towel, you will need 12" length of 1"w flat lace and 12" x 3½" fabric strip.

Fold fabric strip in half lengthwise with wrong sides together and press. Lay stitched piece right side up on flat surface. On cross stitched end, match right sides and align straight edge of lace with short raw edge of stitched piece. Matching raw edges, place fabric strip on top of lace; pin layers together.

Using ¼" seam allowance sew all layers together; remove pins. Using a zigzag stitch, sew over raw edges to prevent fraying. Press seam allowance toward stitched piece.

Press remaining raw edges ⅜" to wrong side; press ⅜" to wrong side again and hem.

Needlework adaptation by Jane Chandler.

Valentine's Day

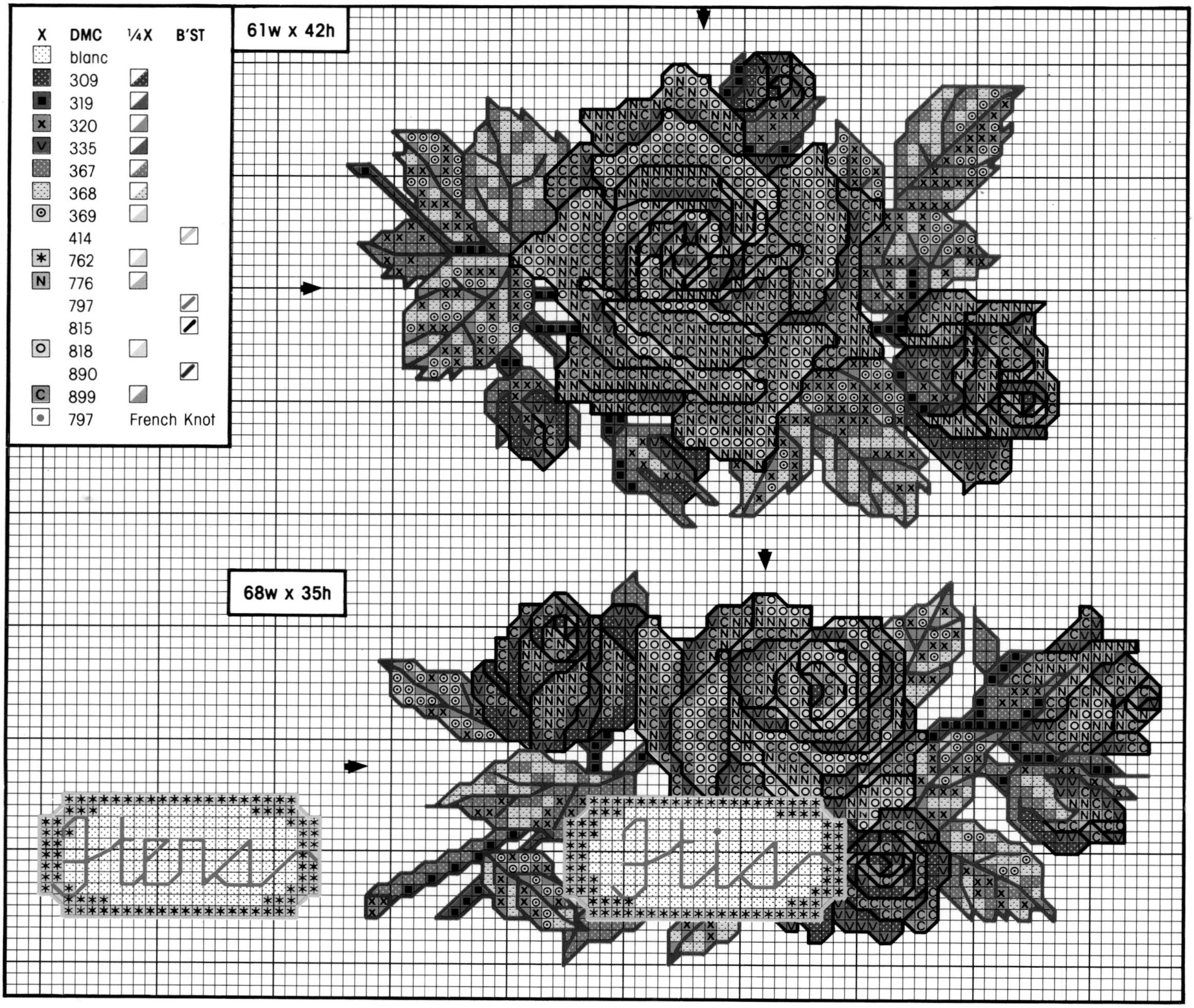

X	DMC	¼X	B'ST
⬚	blanc		
▩	309	◩	
■	319	◩	
x	320	◩	
V	335	◩	
▩	367	◩	
⬚	368	◩	
⊙	369	◩	
	414		⧄
✱	762	◩	
N	776	◩	
	797		⧄
	815		⧄
O	818	◩	
	890		⧄
C	899	◩	
•	797	French Knot	

61w x 42h

68w x 35h

Rose Sheet (shown on page 11): The design was stitched over a 7½" x 5" piece of 13 mesh waste canvas centered on the band of a bed sheet. Three strands of floss were used for Cross Stitch and 1 strand for Backstitch.

His and Hers Pillowcases (shown on page 11): The design was stitched over an 8" x 5" piece of 13 mesh waste canvas centered on the band of a pillowcase. Three strands of floss were used for Cross Stitch, 2 strands for Backstitch words and French Knot, and 1 strand for all other Backstitch.

Needlework adaptation by Jane Chandler.

WORKING ON WASTE CANVAS

Waste canvas is a special canvas that provides an evenweave grid for placing stitches on fabric. After the design is worked over the canvas, the canvas threads are removed leaving the design on the fabric. The canvas is available in several mesh sizes.

Cover edges of canvas with masking tape. (For sweater, cut a piece of lightweight, non-fusible interfacing the same size as canvas to provide a firm stitching base.)

Find desired stitching area and mark center of area with a pin. Match center of canvas to pin. Use the blue threads in canvas to place canvas straight on project; pin canvas to project. (Pin interfacing to wrong side of sweater.) Baste all thicknesses together as shown in **Fig. 1**.

For sweater, place in a screw type hoop. We recommend a hoop that is large enough to encircle entire design.

Using a sharp needle, work design, stitching from large holes to large holes. Trim canvas to within ¾" of design. Dampen canvas until it becomes limp. Pull out canvas threads one at a time using tweezers (**Fig. 2**). Trim interfacing close to design.

Fig. 1

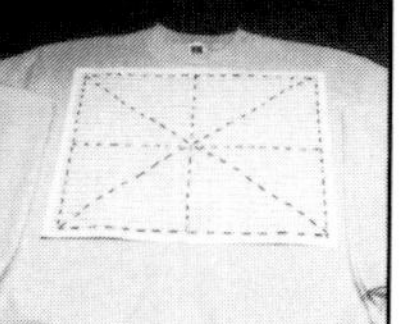

Fig. 2

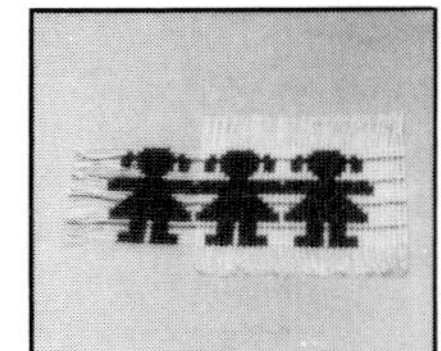

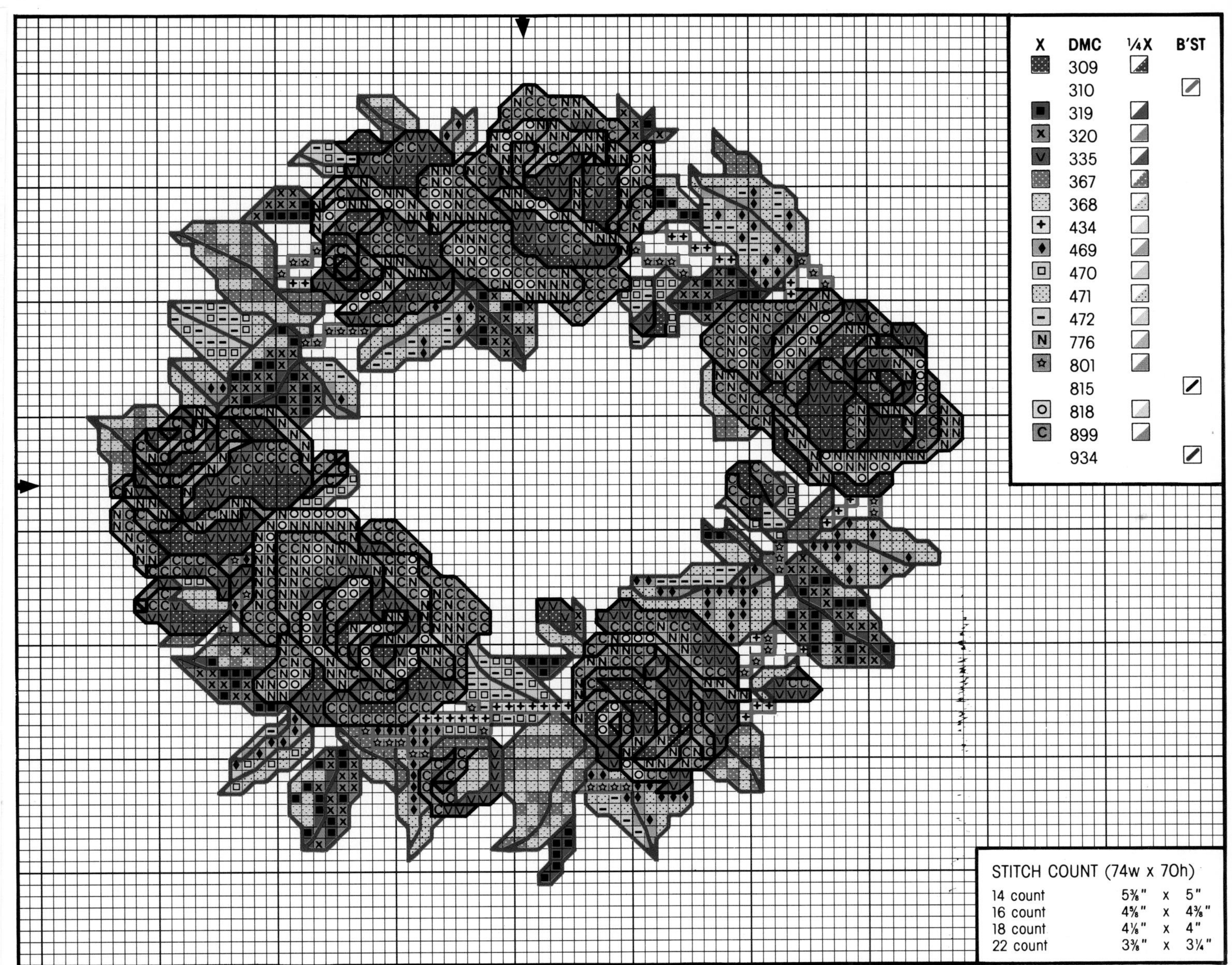

X DMC ¼X B'ST
309
310
319
x 320
V 335
367
368
+ 434
469
470
471
472
N 776
801
815
O 818
C 899
934
STITCH COUNT (74w x 70h)
14 count 5⅜" x 5"
16 count 4⅝" x 4⅜"
18 count 4⅛" x 4"
22 count 3⅜" x 3¼"

Rose Wreath Sweater (shown on page 13): The design was stitched over a 10" square of 12 mesh waste canvas on a purchased sweater. Three strands of floss were used for Cross Stitch, and 1 strand for Backstitch. (See Working on Waste Canvas, page 52.)

Rose Wreath Pillow (shown on page 11): The design was stitched over 2 fabric threads on a 12" square of White Lugana (25 ct). Three strands of floss were used for Cross Stitch and 1 strand for Backstitch.

For pillow, center design and trim stitched piece to measure 10" square. You will also need 10" square of desired fabric for pillow back, 80" length of 2¾"w flat lace, 80" x 6" strip of fabric for ruffle (pieced as necessary), 2" x 42" bias strip of coordinating fabric for cording, 42" length of ¼" dia. purchased cord, and polyester fiberfill.

PILLOW FINISHING

Center cord on wrong side of bias strip; matching long edges, fold strip over cord. Using zipper foot, baste along length of strip close to cord; trim seam allowance to ½". Matching raw edges, pin cording to right side of stitched piece making a ⅜" clip in seam allowance of cording as needed at curves and corners. Ends of cording should overlap approximately 2"; pin overlapping end out of the way. Starting 2" from beginning end of cording and ending 4" from overlapping end, baste cording to stitched piece. On overlapping end of cording, remove 2½" of basting; fold end of fabric back and trim cord so that it meets beginning end of cord. Fold end of fabric under ½"; wrap fabric over beginning end of cording. Finish basting cording to stitched piece.

For fabric and lace ruffle, press short ends of fabric strip ½" to wrong side. Matching wrong sides and long edges, fold strip in half; press. Press short ends of lace ½" to wrong side. Matching raw edge of fabric strip and straight edge of lace, baste layers together close to raw edges. Gather to fit stitched piece. Matching raw edges, pin ruffle to right side of stitched piece overlapping short ends ¼". Using zipper foot and a ½" seam allowance, sew ruffle to stitched piece; remove pins.

Matching right sides and leaving an opening for turning use a ½" seam allowance to sew stitched piece and backing fabric together. Trim seam allowances and clip curves as needed; turn pillow right side out. Stuff pillow with polyester fiberfill and whipstitch opening closed.

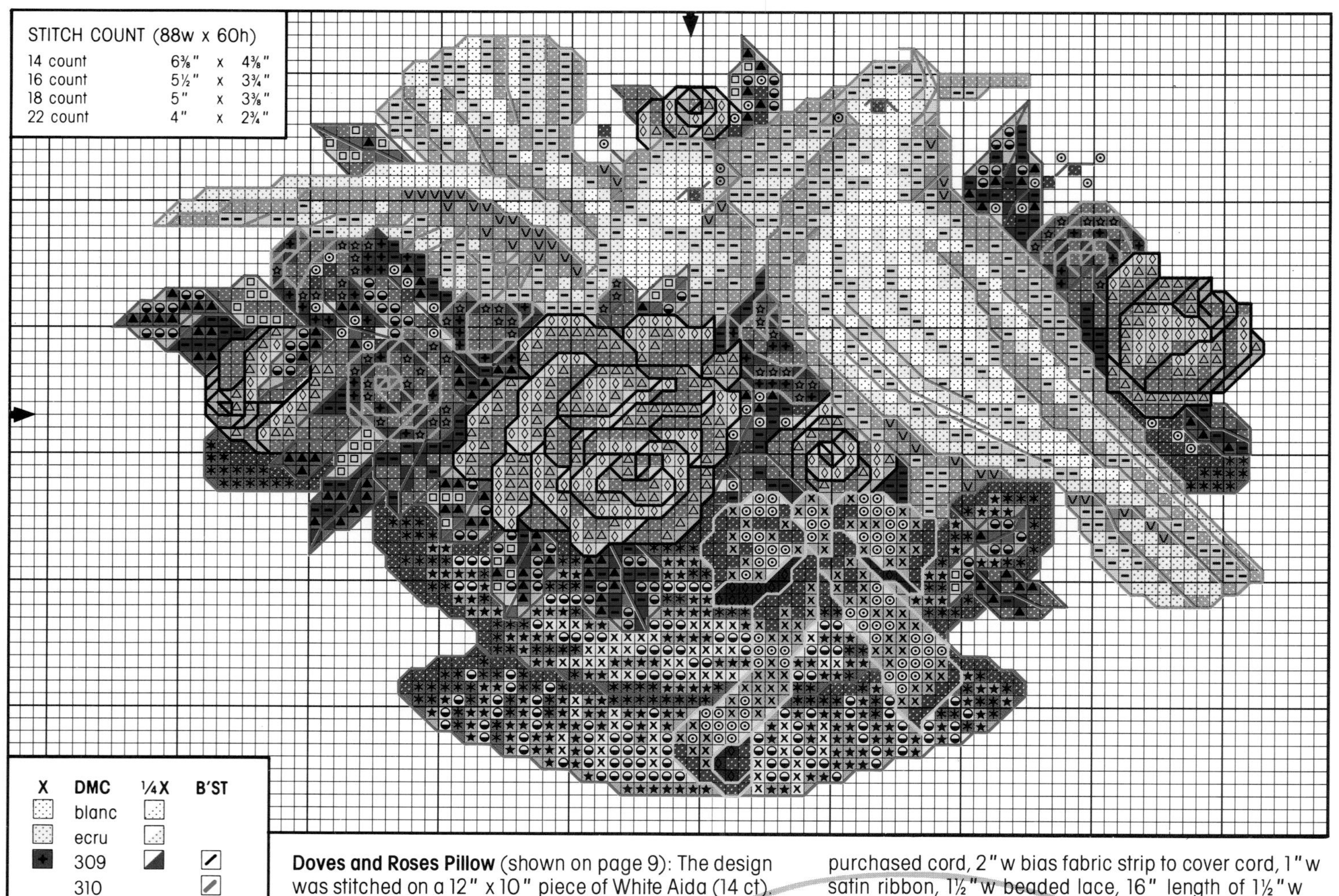

STITCH COUNT (88w x 60h)			
14 count	6⅜"	x	4⅜"
16 count	5½"	x	3¾"
18 count	5"	x	3⅜"
22 count	4"	x	2¾"

X	DMC	¼X	B'ST
✓	blanc	✓	
✓	ecru	✓	
✚	309	✓	✓
	310		✓
	311		✓
◆	312	✓	
–	319	✓	
✓	320	✓	
✓	322	✓	
☆	335	✓	
▲	367	✓	
◒	368	✓	
▫	369	✓	
★	420	✓	
×	422		
V	642	✓	
✓	644	✓	
⊙	729	✓	
△	776	✓	
✓	801	✓	✓
	815		✓
◊	818	✓	
–	822	✓	
✱	869	✓	
	890		✓
✓	899	✓	
◒	3045	✓	
⊙	3325	✓	
×	3755	✓	
	3790		✓

Doves and Roses Pillow (shown on page 9): The design was stitched on a 12" x 10" piece of White Aida (14 ct). Three strands of floss were used for Cross Stitch and 1 strand for Backstitch.

For pillow, you will need tracing paper, 12" x 10" piece of fabric for pillow backing, 48" length of 1¾"w flat lace, 48" x 4" strip of fabric for ruffle (pieced as necessary), 2" x 25" bias strip of coordinating fabric for cording, 25" length of ¼" dia. purchased cord, and polyester fiberfill.

Fold tracing paper in half and match fold to dashed line of heart pattern. Trace pattern onto tracing paper. Leaving paper folded, cut out pattern. Unfold pattern and press flat. With right sides facing and matching raw edges, place stitched piece and backing fabric together. Center pattern on wrong side of stitched piece. Cut out fabric pieces ½" larger than pattern on all sides.

Complete pillow following Pillow Finishing instructions, page 53.

Doves and Roses Keepsake Box (shown on page 12): The design was stitched over 2 fabric threads on a 14" square of White Lugana (25 ct). Three strands of floss were used for Cross Stitch and 1 strand for Backstitch.

Amounts of the following supplies will be determined by size of box. See instructions for determining amounts. You will need a heart-shaped candy box (our box was approx. 9½" x 10"), tracing paper, adhesive board, batting, purchased cord, 2"w bias fabric strip to cover cord, 1"w satin ribbon, 1½"w beaded lace, 16" length of 1½"w satin ribbon for bow, and craft glue.

For pattern, draw around box top on tracing paper; cut out. Draw around pattern on adhesive board; cut out. Pin pattern to batting; cut out and remove pattern. Center pattern over stitched piece and pin in place. Cut stitched piece 1" larger than pattern on all sides; remove pattern. Remove paper from adhesive board and apply batting piece. Center stitched piece right side up on top of batting; smoothly fold and glue edges to back of board, clipping into edges of fabric as needed.

For cording, measure around outside edge of heart-shaped adhesive board and add 2". Cut purchased cord and 2"w bias fabric strip determined measurement. Center cord on wrong side of bias fabric strip; matching long edges, fold strip over cord. Using zipper foot, baste along length of strip close to cord. Referring to photo for placement, glue cording around edge of adhesive board.

Glue 1"w satin ribbon around side of box top. Glue **bead only** of beaded lace around bottom edge of box top. Glue mounted stitched piece to top of box. Tie 1½"w satin ribbon in a bow and trim ends as desired. Refer to photo for placement and glue bow to stitched piece.

Needlework adaptation by Jane Chandler.

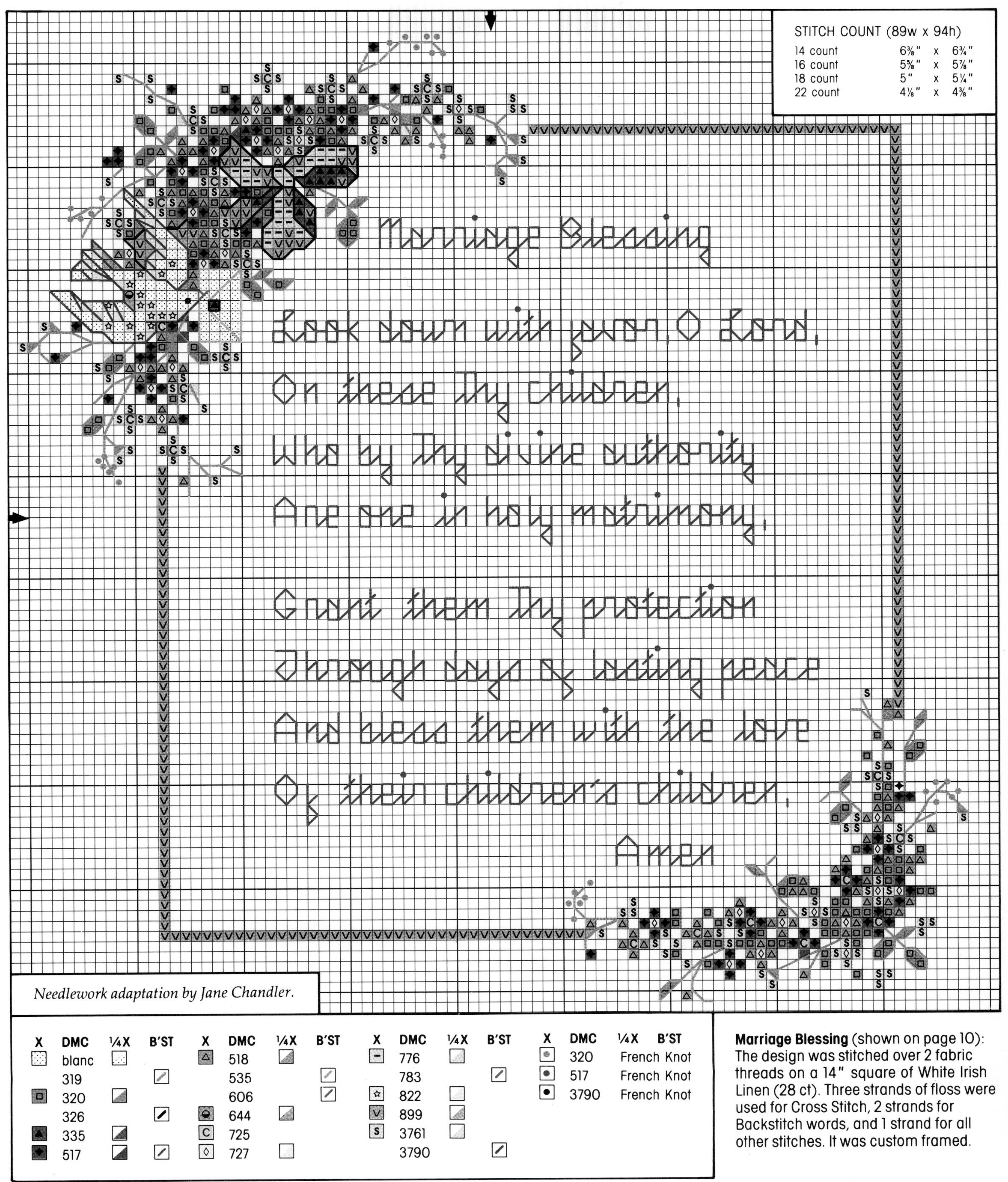

STITCH COUNT (89w x 94h)
14 count 6⅜" x 6¾"
16 count 5⅝" x 5⅞"
18 count 5" x 5¼"
22 count 4⅛" x 4⅜"
Marriage Blessing
Look down with favor, O Lord,
On these Thy children,
Who by Thy divine authority
Are one in holy matrimony,
Grant them Thy protection
Through days of lasting peace
And bless them with the love
Of their children's children,
Amen

Needlework adaptation by Jane Chandler.

X	DMC	¼X	B'ST
⁘	blanc	⁘	
	319		/
▢	320	◪	
	326		/
▲	335	◪	
◆	517	◪	/
△	518	◪	
	535		/
	606		/
◒	644	◪	
C	725		
◊	727	◻	
−	776	◻	
	783		/
☆	822	◻	
V	899	◪	
S	3761	◻	
	3790		/
●	320	French Knot	
●	517	French Knot	
●	3790	French Knot	

Marriage Blessing (shown on page 10): The design was stitched over 2 fabric threads on a 14" square of White Irish Linen (28 ct). Three strands of floss were used for Cross Stitch, 2 strands for Backstitch words, and 1 strand for all other stitches. It was custom framed.

Presidents' Day

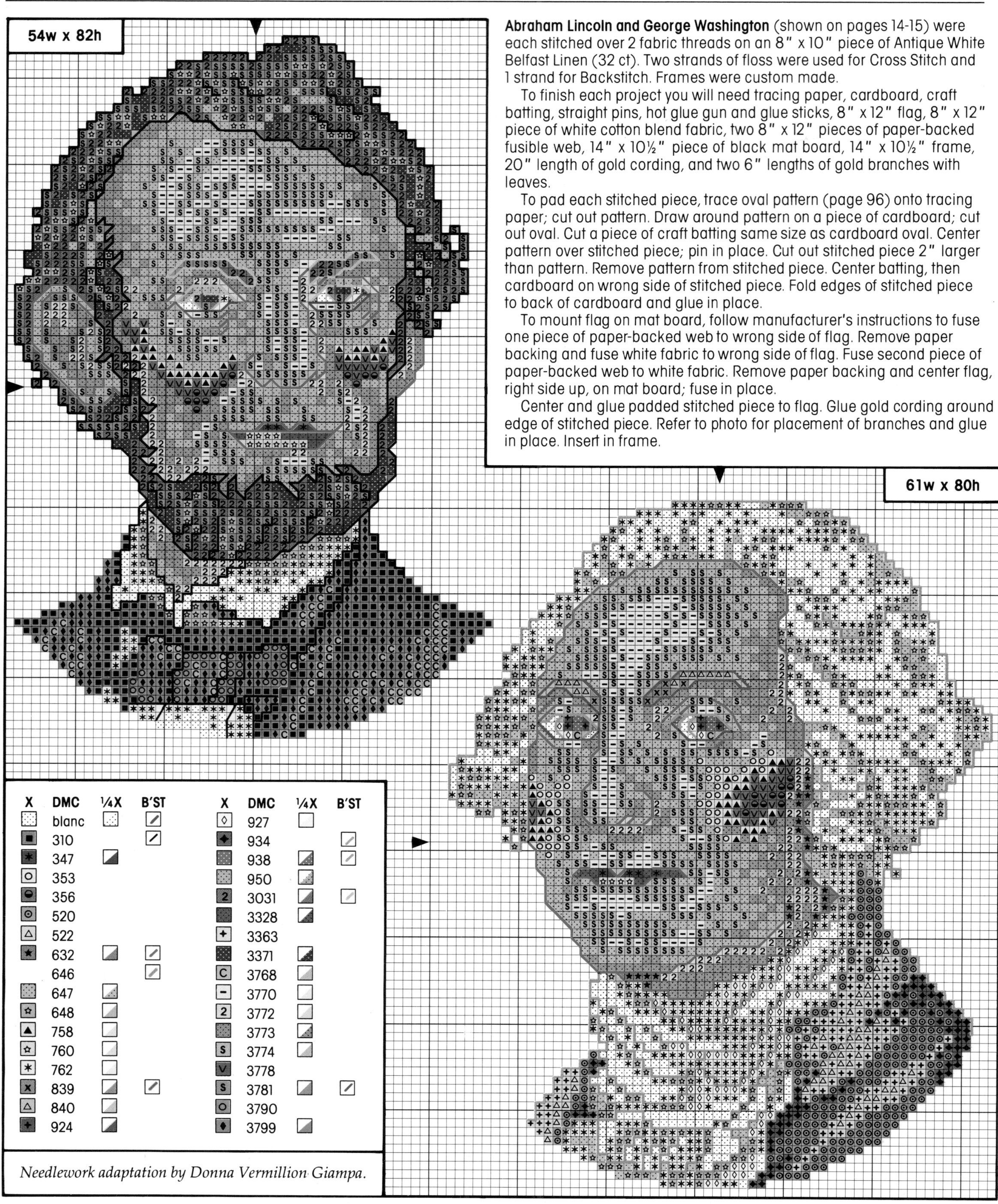

Abraham Lincoln and George Washington (shown on pages 14-15) were each stitched over 2 fabric threads on an 8" x 10" piece of Antique White Belfast Linen (32 ct). Two strands of floss were used for Cross Stitch and 1 strand for Backstitch. Frames were custom made.

To finish each project you will need tracing paper, cardboard, craft batting, straight pins, hot glue gun and glue sticks, 8" x 12" flag, 8" x 12" piece of white cotton blend fabric, two 8" x 12" pieces of paper-backed fusible web, 14" x 10½" piece of black mat board, 14" x 10½" frame, 20" length of gold cording, and two 6" lengths of gold branches with leaves.

To pad each stitched piece, trace oval pattern (page 96) onto tracing paper; cut out pattern. Draw around pattern on a piece of cardboard; cut out oval. Cut a piece of craft batting same size as cardboard oval. Center pattern over stitched piece; pin in place. Cut out stitched piece 2" larger than pattern. Remove pattern from stitched piece. Center batting, then cardboard on wrong side of stitched piece. Fold edges of stitched piece to back of cardboard and glue in place.

To mount flag on mat board, follow manufacturer's instructions to fuse one piece of paper-backed web to wrong side of flag. Remove paper backing and fuse white fabric to wrong side of flag. Fuse second piece of paper-backed web to white fabric. Remove paper backing and center flag, right side up, on mat board; fuse in place.

Center and glue padded stitched piece to flag. Glue gold cording around edge of stitched piece. Refer to photo for placement of branches and glue in place. Insert in frame.

X	DMC	¼X	B'ST	X	DMC	¼X	B'ST
	blanc	✓	✓	◊	927	✓	
■	310		✓	♦	934		✓
✱	347	✓			938	✓	✓
O	353				950	✓	
	356			2	3031	✓	✓
⊙	520				3328	✓	
△	522			+	3363		
★	632	✓	✓		3371	✓	
	646		✓	C	3768	✓	
	647	✓		-	3770	✓	
☆	648	✓		2	3772	✓	
▲	758	✓			3773	✓	
☆	760	✓		S	3774	✓	
✱	762	✓		V	3778		
×	839	✓	✓	S	3781	✓	✓
△	840	✓		O	3790		
+	924	✓		♦	3799	✓	

Needlework adaptation by Donna Vermillion Giampa.

St. Patrick's Day

May the most
you wish for
Be the least
you get.
May the best times
you've ever had
Be the worst
you will ever see.
OLD CELTIC BLESSING

X	DMC	¼X	B'ST
⋯	blanc	⋯	
◒ *	319 & 367	◢	
S †	319 & 890	◢	
×	320	◢	
−	368	◢	
	414		⁄
□	469	◢	
▒	470	◢	
+	471	◢	
△	472	◢	
	890		⁄
	930		⁄ ★
○	931	◢	
●	930	French Knot	

* Use 1 strand of 319 and 2 strands of 367.
† Use 2 strands of 319 and 1 strand of 890.
★ Use 2 strands for words.

Celtic Blessing (shown on page 17) was stitched over 2 fabric threads on a 15" x 16" piece of Antique White Dublin Linen (25 ct). Three strands of floss were used for Cross Stitch, 2 strands for Backstitch words and French Knots, and 1 strand for all other Backstitch. It was custom framed.

Designed by Nancy Dockter.

STITCH COUNT (91w x 98h)

14 count	6½"	x	7"
16 count	5¾"	x	6⅛"
18 count	5⅛"	x	5½"
22 count	4¼"	x	4½"

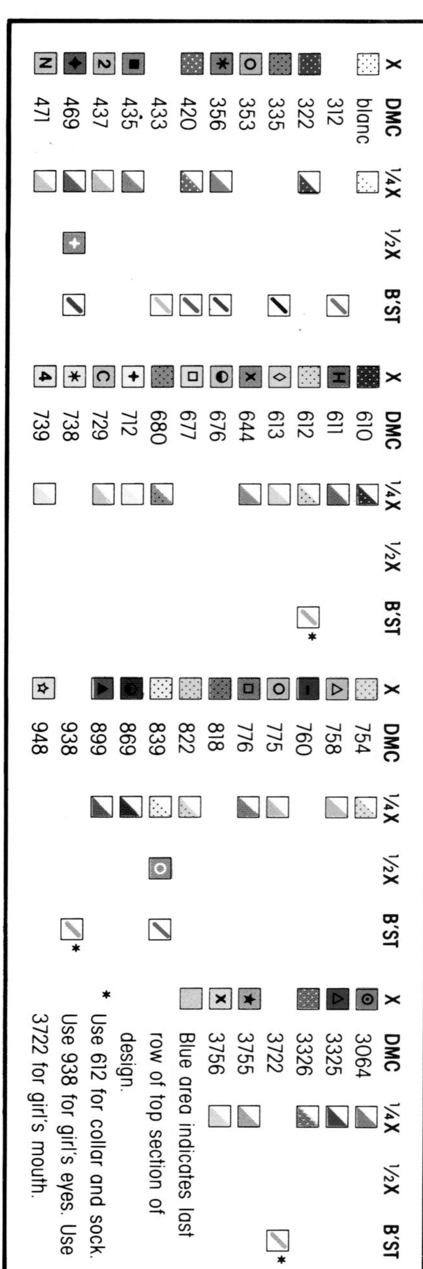

DMC	¼X	½X	B'ST
blanc	✓		
312			✓
322	✓		
335			✓
353			
356	✓		✓
420	✓		✓
433			✓
435	✓		
437	✓		
469	✓	✓	✓
471	✓		
610	✓		
611	✓		
612	✓		✓*
613	✓		
644	✓		
676			
677			
680	✓		
712	✓		
729	✓		
738			
739	✓		
754	✓		
758	✓		
760			
775	✓		
776	✓		
818			
822	✓		
839	✓	✓	✓
869	✓		
899	✓		
938			✓*
948			
3064	✓		
3325	✓		
3326	✓		
3722			✓*
3755	✓		
3756	✓		

Blue area indicates last row of top section of design.

* Use 612 for collar and sock. Use 938 for girl's eyes. Use 3722 for girl's mouth.

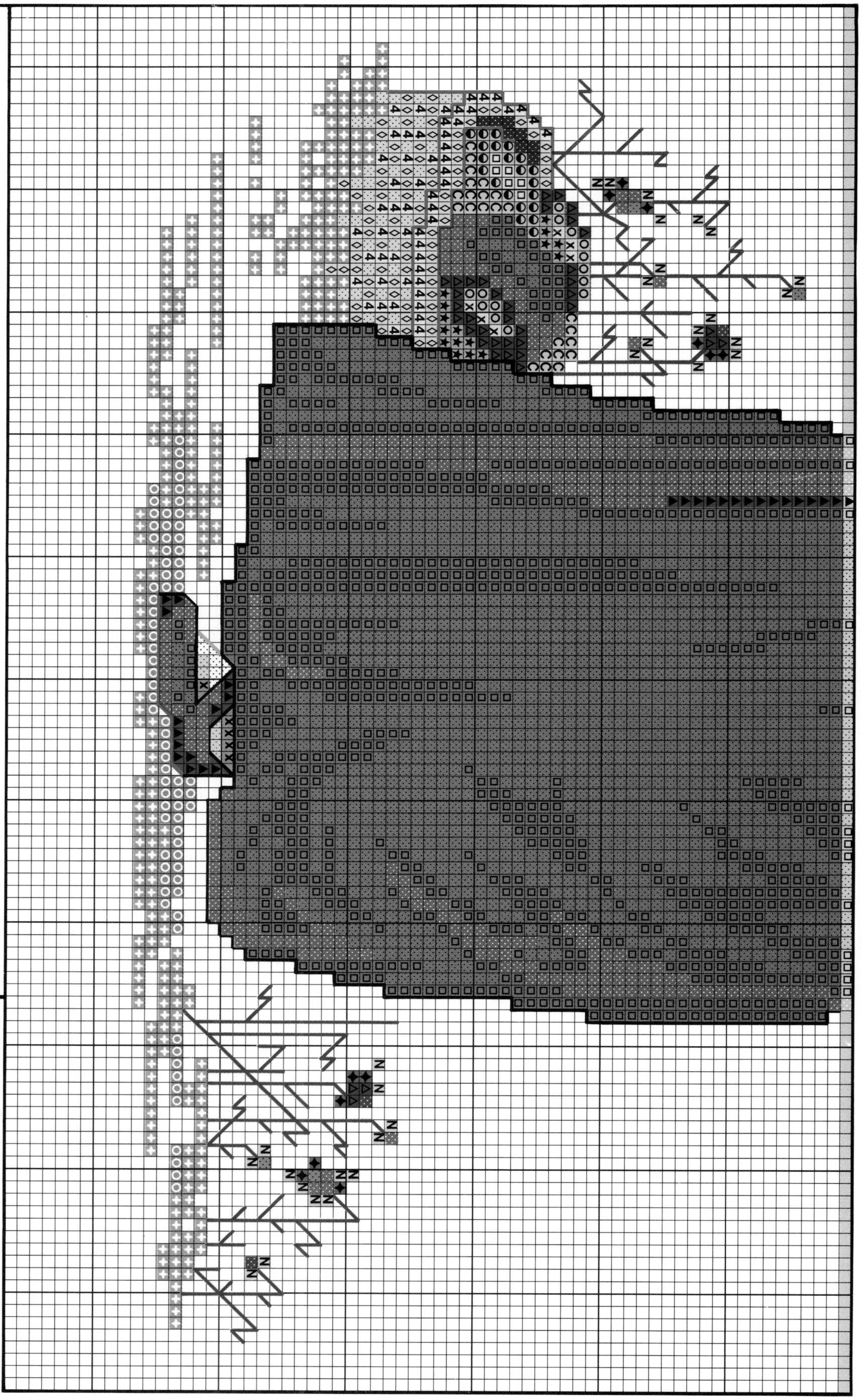

Easter Bonnet Girl (shown on page 19) was stitched over 2 fabric threads on a 14" x 16" piece of White Lugana (25 ct). Two strands of floss were used for Cross Stitch and 1 strand for Half Cross Stitch and Backstitch. It was custom framed.

Needlework adaptation by Carol Emmer.

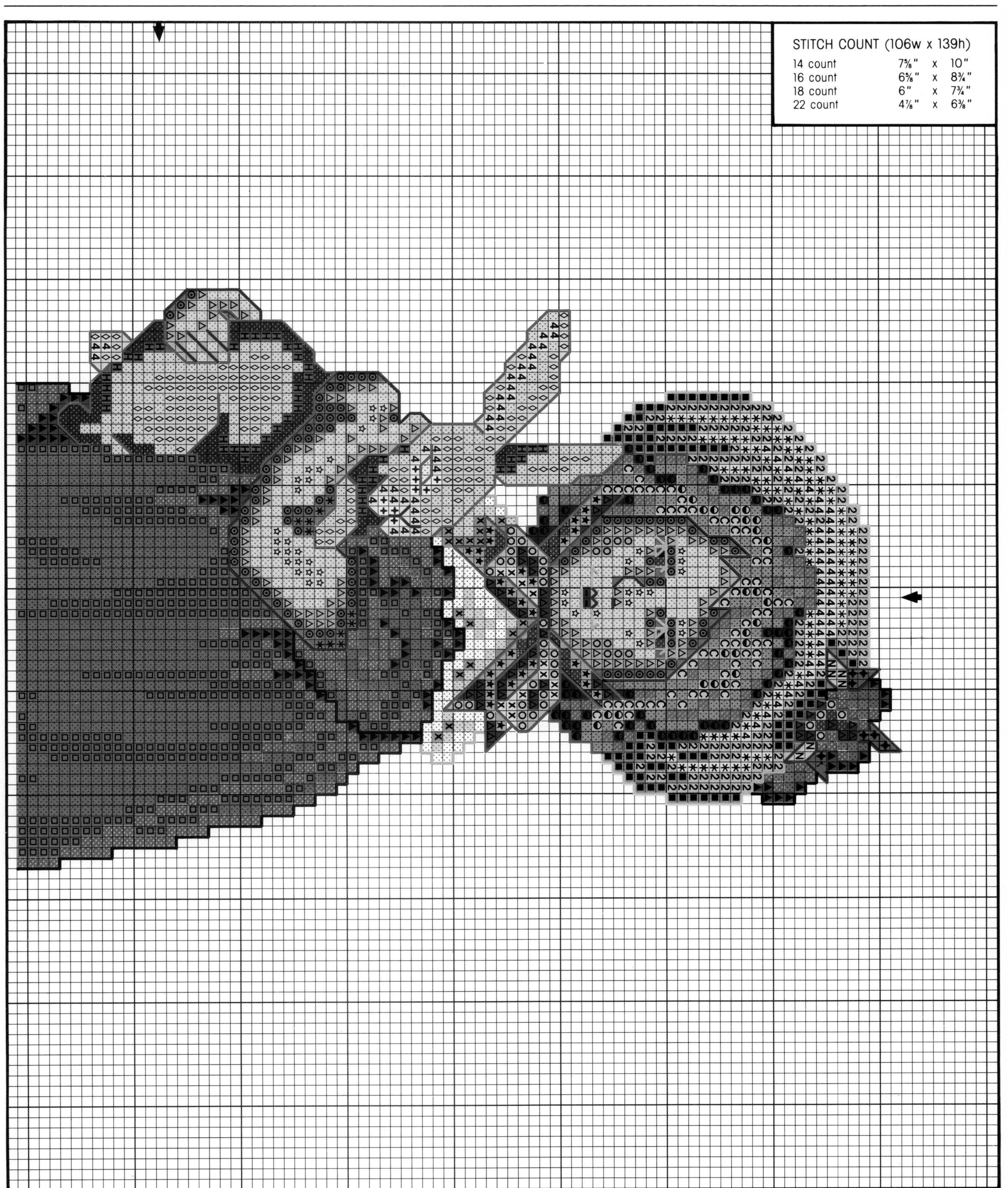
STITCH COUNT (106w x 139h)
14 count 7⅝" x 10"
16 count 6⅝" x 8¾"
18 count 6" x 7¾"
22 count 4⅞" x 6⅜"

Flower Girls (shown on page 22): Each design was stitched on a 6" square of Ivory Aida (18 ct). Two strands of floss were used for Cross Stitch and 1 strand for Backstitch. They were inserted in artificial flowers.

Trace pattern onto tracing paper; cut out pattern. For each Flower Girl, center pattern on right side of stitched piece and draw around pattern; cut out. Thread needle with a 20" length of six-strand embroidery floss and baste ½" from raw edge of stitched piece. Pull ends of floss to gather stitched piece; firmly stuff with polyester fiberfill. Pull floss ends tight and knot to secure. Apply a generous amount of liquid fray preventative to raw edges of stitched piece (up to basting line); allow to dry. Trim raw edges ⅛" from basting line; clip excess floss ends.

If necessary, remove center of artificial flower. Refer to photo and hot glue stitched piece to inside center of flower.

Designed by Carol Emmer.

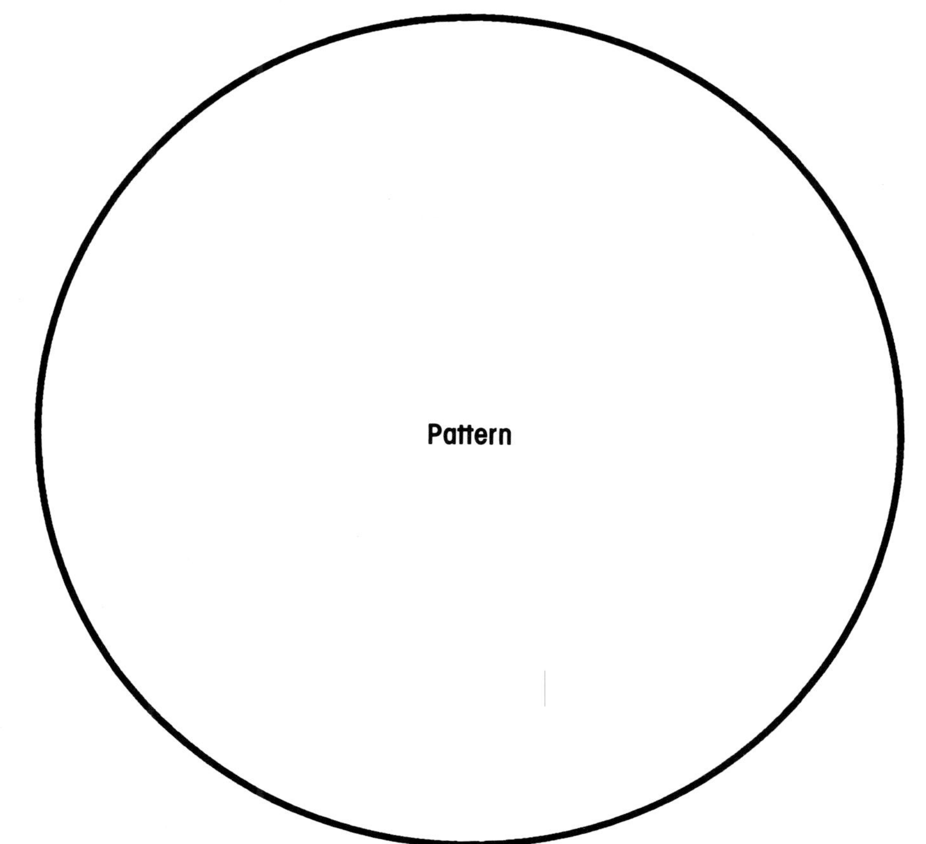

X	DMC	¼X	¾X	B'ST
×	353			
	356			■
■	420	■		
N	422	■		
C	433	■		
■	434	■		■
+	435	■		
■	436			
△	437			
◊	754	■		
−	758	■		
☆	760			
■	801	■		■
	839			■
♦	869	■		■
⊙	931		■	
■	948	■		
■	3045			
■	3064	■		
	3722			■

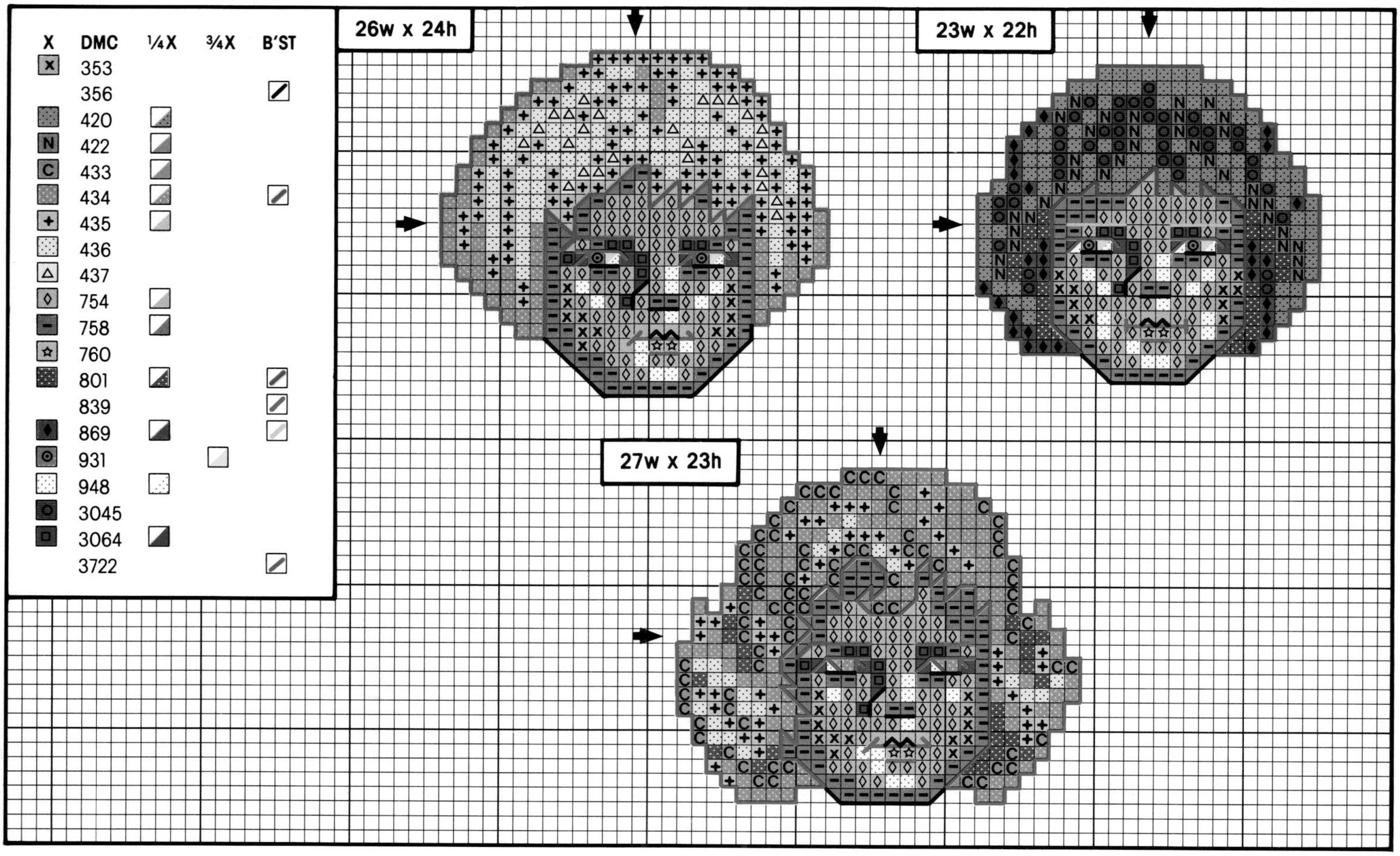

26w x 24h

23w x 22h

27w x 23h

STITCH COUNT (83w x 52h)			
14 count	6"	x	3 3/4"
16 count	5 1/4"	x	3 1/4"
18 count	4 5/8"	x	3"
22 count	3 7/8"	x	2 3/8"

X	DMC	1/4X	1/2X	B'ST
■	blanc	■		
	310			■
+	319			
⊙	320			
♦	322			■
■	347			
x	368			
C	433	■		
■	434			
▲	680	■		
-	712			
2	729	■		
+	738			
△	739			
□	743	■		
■	744			
♦	745			
☆	760			
⊙	761			
	801			■
	815			■
	890			■
+	3325			
4	3328			■
◒	3346		■	
□	3347			
x	3712			
◊	3713			
V	3755			
■	801 Lazy Daisy			

Chick in Frame (shown on page 21): The design was stitched over 2 fabric threads on a 12" x 10" piece of White Belfast Linen (32 ct). Two strands of floss were used for Cross Stitch and 1 strand for all other stitches. It was custom framed.

Chick Sweater (shown on page 23): The design was stitched over an 11" x 8" piece of 12 mesh waste canvas on a purchased sweater with top of design approx. 1 1/2" below bottom of neckband. Three strands of floss were used for Cross Stitch and 1 strand for all other stitches.

Needlework adaptation by Jane Chandler.

WORKING ON WASTE CANVAS

Waste canvas is a special canvas that provides an evenweave grid for placing stitches on fabric. After the design is worked over the canvas, the canvas threads are removed leaving the design on the fabric. The canvas is available in several mesh sizes.

Cover edges of canvas with masking tape. Cut a piece of lightweight, non-fusible interfacing the same size as canvas to provide a firm stitching base.

Find desired stitching area on sweater and mark center of area with a pin. Match center of canvas to pin. Use the blue threads in canvas to place canvas straight on sweater; pin canvas to sweater. Pin interfacing to wrong side of sweater. Baste all three thicknesses together as shown in **Fig. 1**.

Place sweater in a screw type hoop. We recommend a hoop that is large enough to encircle entire design. Using a sharp needle, work design, stitching from large holes to large holes.

Trim canvas to within 3/4" of design. Dampen canvas until it becomes limp. Pull out canvas threads one at a time using tweezers (**Fig. 2**). Trim interfacing close to design.

Fig. 1

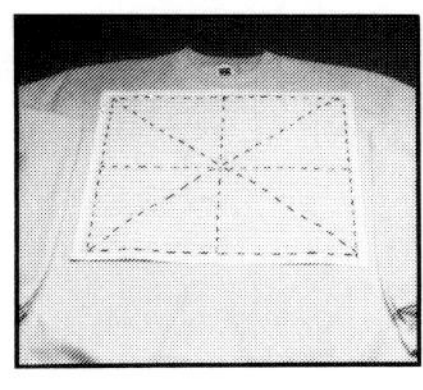

Fig. 2

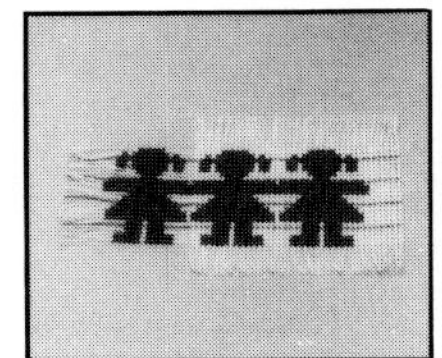

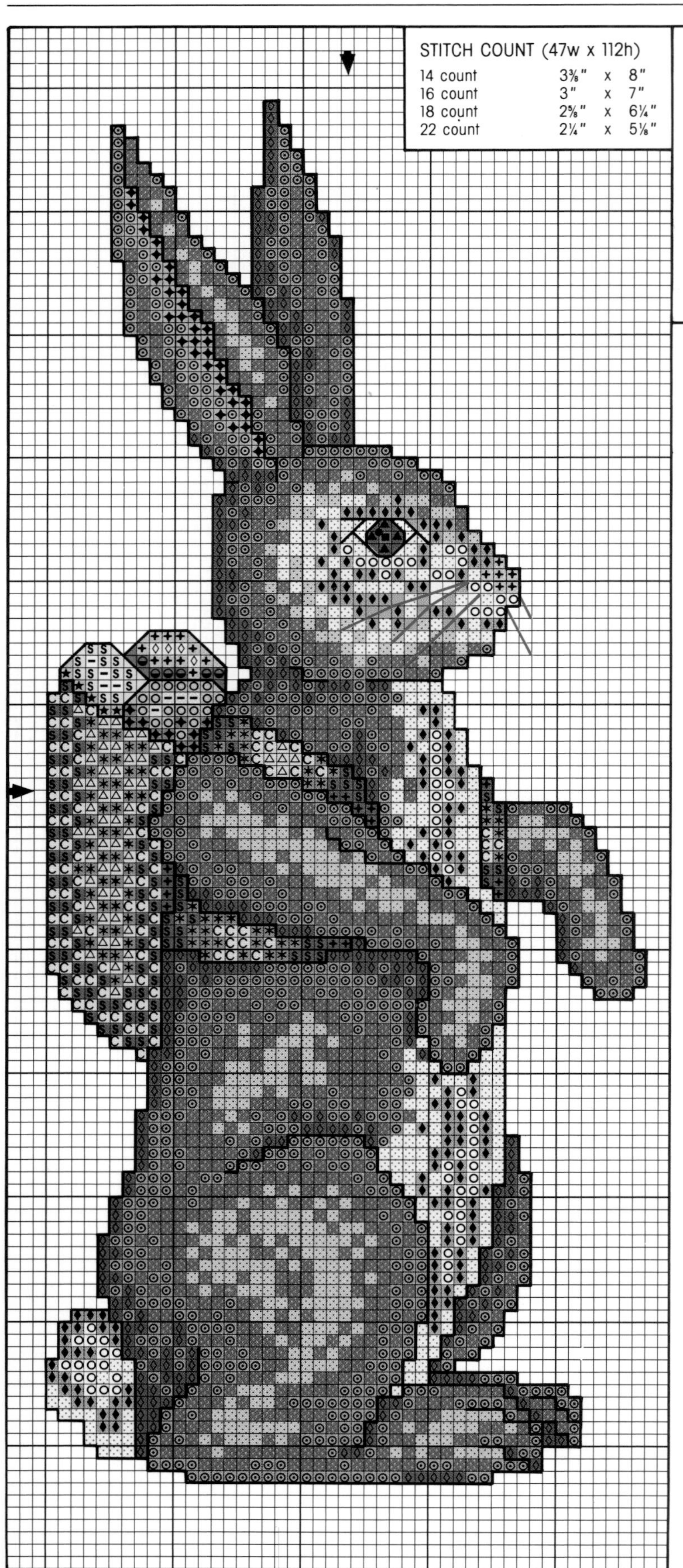

STITCH COUNT (47w x 112h)			
14 count	3⅜"	x	8"
16 count	3"	x	7"
18 count	2⅝"	x	6¼"
22 count	2¼"	x	5⅛"

X	DMC	¼X	B'ST	X	DMC	¼X	X	DMC	¼X	B'ST
	blanc				743			3045		
	ecru			S	744		C	3046		
	310			−	745		△	3047		
S	420				754			3325		
	433				758			3712		
	434				760			3755		
	435			◊	761			3781		*
	436			−	775			blanc	French Knot	
	738				869		*	Work in long stitches.		
	739				3031					

Bunny Figure (shown on page 23): The design was stitched on a 9" x 15" piece of Ivory Aida (11 ct). Four strands of floss were used for Cross Stitch and 2 strands for Backstitch and French Knot. It was made into a stuffed figure.

For stuffed figure, cut a piece of Aida same size as stitched piece for backing. Matching right sides and raw edges and leaving bottom edge open, sew stitched piece and backing fabric together ¼" from design. Trim excess fabric leaving a ¼" seam allowance. Clip seam allowances at curves; turn figure right side out and carefully push curves outward. Trim bottom edge of figure ½" from bottom of design. Press raw edges ¼" to wrong side; stuff figure with polyester fiberfill up to 1½" from opening.

For base, set figure on tracing paper and draw around base of figure. Add a ½" seam allowance to pattern; cut out. Place pattern on a piece of Aida. Use fabric marking pencil to draw around pattern; cut out along drawn line. Baste around base piece ½" from raw edge; press raw edges to wrong side along basting line.

To weight bottom of figure, fill a plastic sandwich bag with a small amount of aquarium gravel. Place bag of gravel into bottom of figure.

Pin wrong side of base piece over opening. Whipstitch in place, adding polyester fiberfill as necessary to fill bottom of figure. Remove basting threads.

Bunny Sweater (shown on page 23): The design was stitched over a 7½" x 13" piece of 11 mesh waste canvas on a purchased cardigan. Four strands of floss were used for Cross Stitch and 2 strands for Backstitch and French Knot. (See Working on Waste Canvas, page 61.)

Designed by Jane Chandler.

Girl and Bunny Hat Box (shown on page 20): The design was stitched over 2 fabric threads on a 14" square of White Lugana (25 ct). Three strands of floss were used for Cross Stitch and 1 strand for Backstitch. It was applied to the lid of a hat box.

For lid, cut a paper pattern 1" larger on all sides than box lid. Centering pattern on design, cut out stitched piece. Clip ⅜" into edge of stitched piece at 1" intervals. Cut batting same size as lid; place batting on lid. Place stitched piece on batting; fold edge of stitched piece down and glue to side of lid. Layer and glue ribbon around side of lid in the following order: ⅞"w satin ribbon, ½"w satin ribbon, and ¼"w grosgrain ribbon.

Needlework adaptation by Carol Emmer.

STITCH COUNT (82w x 91h)

14 count	5⅞"	x	6½"
16 count	5⅛"	x	5¾"
18 count	4⅝"	x	5⅛"
22 count	3¾"	x	4¼"

X	DMC	¼X	¾X	B'ST
	blanc			*
	301			
	322			†
	353			
	356			
	435			
	632			
	640			
*	642			*
C	644			
x	676			
O	677			
△	729			
V	754			
	758			*
	760			
V	775			
	801			
S	822			
	838			*
	839			
	869			
	931			†
	932			
-	948			
	3064			
O	3325			
	3712			
	3722			*
	3755			
-	3756			
	3770			
	3772			

* Use blanc for bunny's brow whiskers (work in long stitches). Use 642 for lace on girl's dress. Use 758 for bunny's nose. Use 838 for girl's eyes. Use 3722 for girl's mouth.

† Use 322 for bow on girl's dress. Use 931 for girl's eyes.

Easter

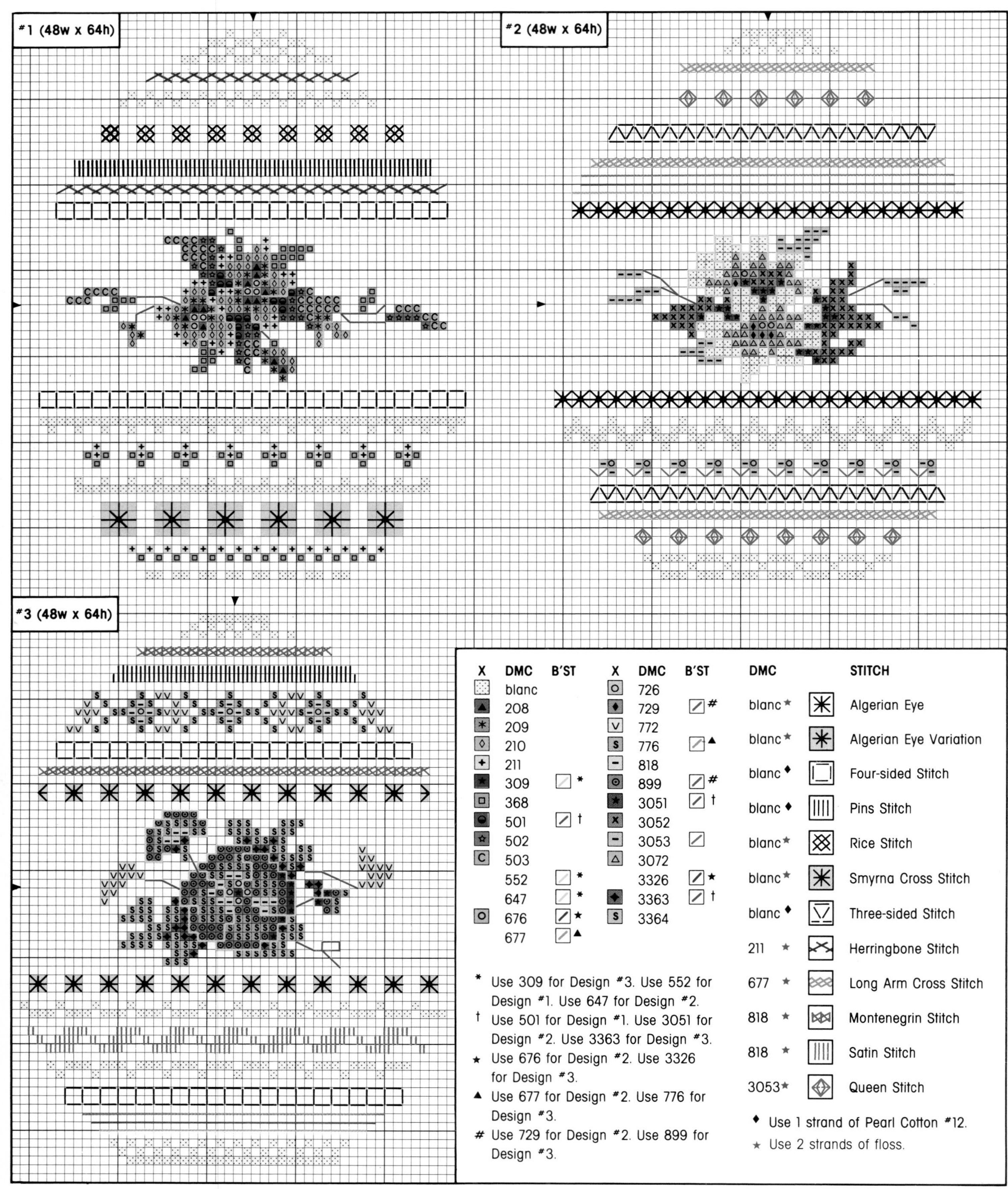

#1 (48w x 64h)
#2 (48w x 64h)
#3 (48w x 64h)
X DMC B'ST
blanc
208
209
210
211
309 *
368
501 †
502
503
552 *
647 *
676 ★
677 ▲
X DMC B'ST
726
729 #
772
776 ▲
818
899 #
3051 †
3052
3053
3072
3326 ★
3363 †
3364
DMC STITCH
blanc ★ Algerian Eye
blanc ★ Algerian Eye Variation
blanc ♦ Four-sided Stitch
blanc ♦ Pins Stitch
blanc ★ Rice Stitch
blanc ★ Smyrna Cross Stitch
blanc ♦ Three-sided Stitch
211 ★ Herringbone Stitch
677 ★ Long Arm Cross Stitch
818 ★ Montenegrin Stitch
818 ★ Satin Stitch
3053 ★ Queen Stitch
* Use 309 for Design #3. Use 552 for Design #1. Use 647 for Design #2.
† Use 501 for Design #1. Use 3051 for Design #2. Use 3363 for Design #3.
★ Use 676 for Design #2. Use 3326 for Design #3.
▲ Use 677 for Design #2. Use 776 for Design #3.
Use 729 for Design #2. Use 899 for Design #3.
♦ Use 1 strand of Pearl Cotton #12.
★ Use 2 strands of floss.

Egg Ornaments (shown on page 21): Each design was stitched over 2 fabric threads on a 6" x 8" piece of White Belfast Linen (32 ct). Two strands of floss were used for Cross Stitch and 1 strand for Backstitch. Refer to chart for number of strands to use for Embroidery and Pulled Stitches.

For each ornament, you will need 4" Styrofoam® egg, 6" x 8" piece of Belfast Linen for back, craft glue, T-pins, 18" length of 1"w wire-edged ribbon, 18" length of satin cord, and 13" lengths of the following: 7/8"w satin ribbon, 1/2"w satin ribbon, and 1/2"w decorative trim.

Using outside edge of design as guide, trim stitched piece in oval shape 1/2" larger on all sides than design. Cut backing fabric same size as stitched piece. Apply glue to wrong side of backing fabric and position on egg smoothing wrinkles and easing excess fabric at sides. Stick T-pins into egg around raw edges of fabric to hold in place. Repeat for stitched piece. Remove T-pins when glue has dried. Center and glue trims around egg over raw edges in the following order: 7/8"w ribbon, 1/2"w ribbon, and 1/2"w trim.

Use 1"w wire-edged ribbon to make bow. Glue bow to top of ornament. For hanger, glue each end of satin cord to top of ornament behind bow.

Violet Collar Point (shown on page 20): The violet from Design #1 was stitched over a 3" square of 16 mesh waste canvas on the collar point of a purchased blouse. Two strands of floss were used for Cross Stitch and 1 strand for Backstitch. (See Working on Waste Canvas, page 52.)

Designed by Linda Culp Calhoun.

EMBROIDERY STITCHES

(**Note:** For Figs. with numbered stitches, come up at 1 and all odd numbers; go down at 2 and all even numbers.)

Herringbone Stitch: This overlapping stitch is worked continuously from left to right. Complete first stitch (stitches 1-4); then work next stitch (stitches 5-8) as shown in **Fig. 1**. Work all consecutive stitches in the same manner as stitches 5-8.

Fig. 1

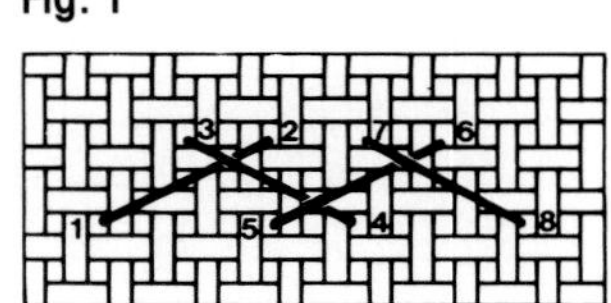

Long Arm Cross Stitch: This overlapping stitch is worked continuously from left to right. Complete first stitch (stitches 1-4); then work next stitch (stitches 5-8) as shown in **Fig. 2**. Work all consecutive stitches in the same manner as stitches 5-8.

Fig. 2

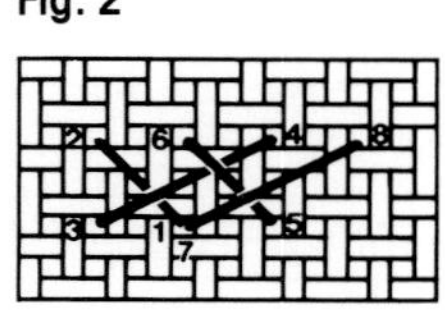

Montenegrin Stitch: This overlapping stitch is worked continuously from left to right. Complete first stitch (stitches 1-6) as shown in **Fig. 3a**; then work next stitch (stitches 7-12) (**Fig. 3b**). Work all consecutive stitches in the same manner as stitches 7-12.

Fig. 3a

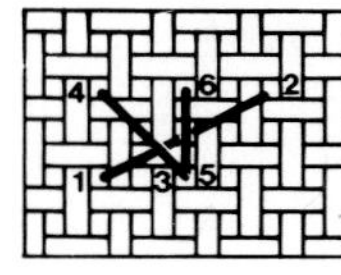

Fig. 3b

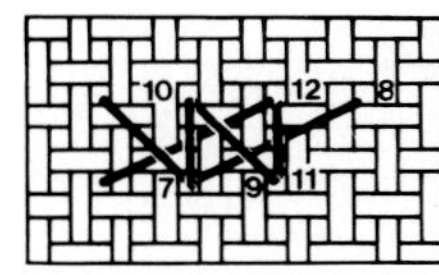

Queen Stitch: This decorative stitch forms a diamond shape. Pull a long stitch (stitch 1-2) loosely and catch with a short stitch (stitch 3-4) (**Fig. 4a**). Complete stitch (stitches 5-16), catching each long stitch with a short stitch as shown in **Figs. 4a-c**.

Fig. 4a

Fig. 4b **Fig. 4c**

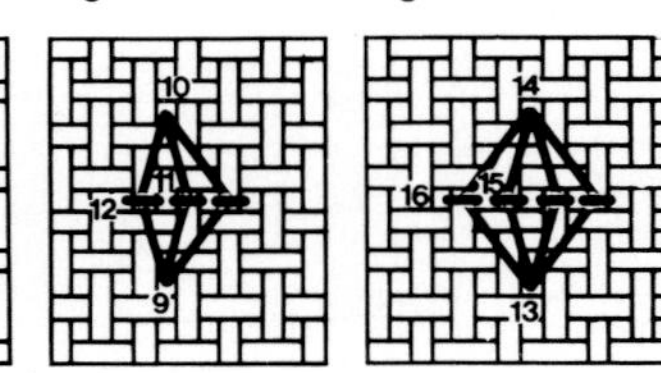

Rice Stitch: This decorative stitch is formed by first working a large Cross Stitch (stitches 1-4) and then working a stitch over each leg of the Cross Stitch (stitches 5-12) as shown in **Fig. 5**.

Fig. 5

Satin Stitch: This stitch is a series of straight stitches worked side by side (**Fig. 6**). The number of threads worked over and the direction of stitches will vary according to the chart.

Fig. 6

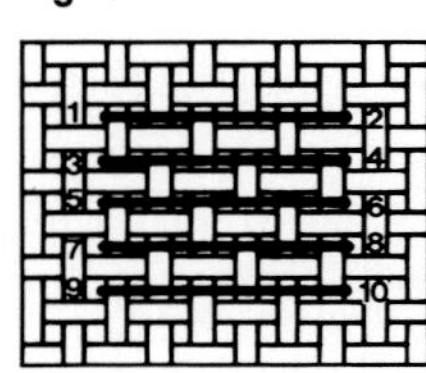

Smyrna Cross Stitch: This decorative stitch is formed by working four stitches (stitches 1-8) as shown in **Fig. 7**. The top stitch (stitch 7-8) of all Smyrna Cross Stitches must be made in the same direction.

Fig. 7

PULLED STITCHES

Fabric threads should be pulled tightly together to create an opening in the fabric around the stitch. Figs. show placement of stitch but do not show pulling of the fabric threads. Keep tension even throughout work.

Algerian Eye Stitch: An "eye" is formed in the center of this stitch. Come up at 1, go down in center, and pull tightly toward 3. Come up at 3, go down in center, and pull tightly toward 5; continue working in this manner until stitch is complete (stitches 5-15) (**Fig. 8**). Work row of Algerian Eye Stitches from right to left.

Fig. 8

Four-sided Stitch: This continuous stitch is worked from left to right. Come up at 1 and pull tightly toward 2; then go down at 2 and pull tightly toward 1. Work stitches 3-14 in same manner (**Fig. 9**). Continue working in the same manner to end of row.

Fig. 9

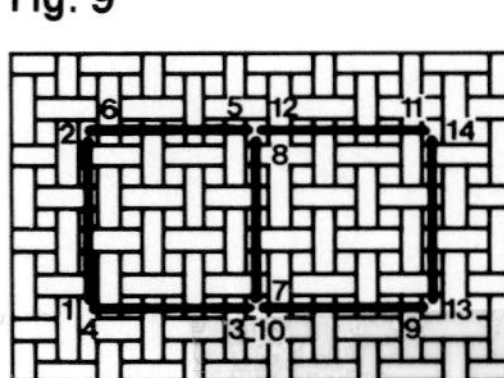

Pins Stitch: This stitch is a series of straight stitches worked side by side (**Fig. 10**). Complete stitch 1-2, come up at 3, and pull tightly; go down at 4, come up at 5, and pull tightly. Continue working in the same manner to end of row.

Fig. 10

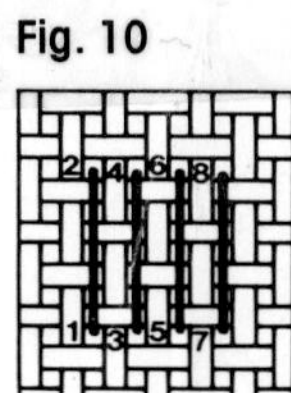

Three-sided Stitch: This continuous stitch is worked from right to left. Each stitch is worked twice; stitches 1-2 and 3-4 are over the same fabric threads (**Fig. 11a**). Come up at 1 and pull tightly toward 2; then go down at 2 and pull tightly toward 1. Work stitch 3-4 over the same fabric threads. Work stitches 5-22 in same manner (**Figs. 11a-c**). Continue working in the same manner to end of row.

Fig. 11a

Fig. 11b

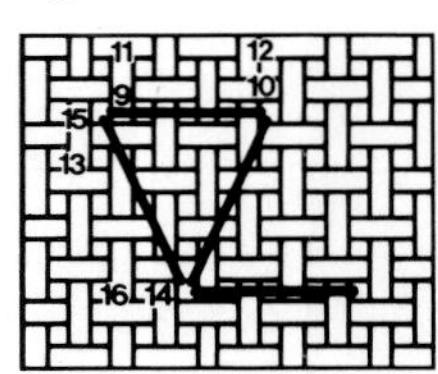

Fig. 11c

Memorial Day

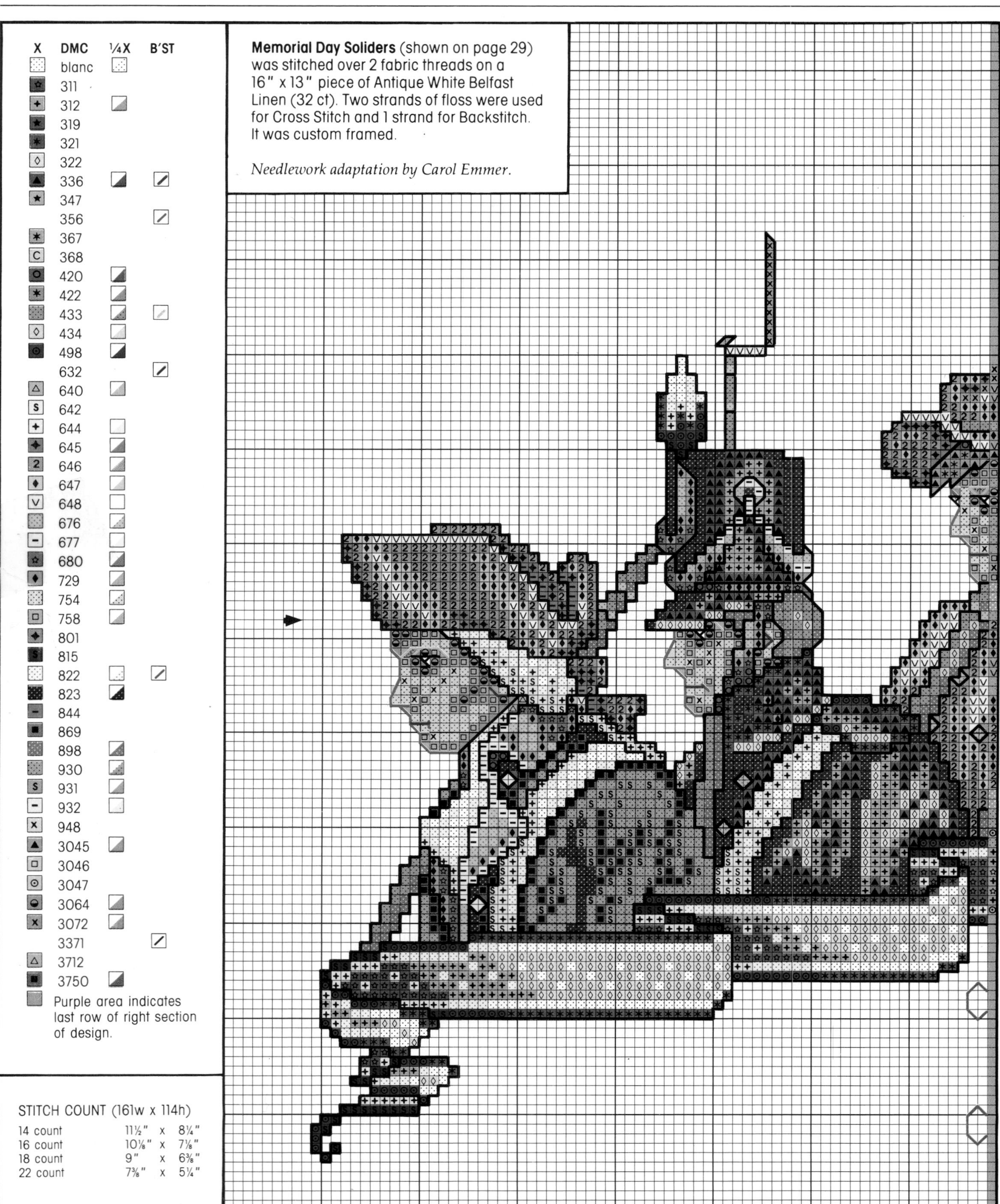

Memorial Day Soliders (shown on page 29) was stitched over 2 fabric threads on a 16" x 13" piece of Antique White Belfast Linen (32 ct). Two strands of floss were used for Cross Stitch and 1 strand for Backstitch. It was custom framed.

Needlework adaptation by Carol Emmer.

STITCH COUNT (161w x 114h)

14 count	11½"	x	8¼"
16 count	10⅛"	x	7⅛"
18 count	9"	x	6⅜"
22 count	7⅜"	x	5¼"